CULTURE SHOCK!
Korea

Sonja Vegdahl &
Ben Seunghwa Hur

Graphic Arts Center Publishing Company
Portland, Oregon

In the same series

Argentina	Ecuador	Laos	South Africa
Australia	Egypt	Malaysia	Spain
Austria	Finland	Mauritius	Sri Lanka
Belgium	France	Mexico	Sweden
Bolivia	Germany	Morocco	Switzerland
Borneo	Greece	Myanmar	Syria
Brazil	Hong Kong	Nepal	Taiwan
Britain	Hungary	Netherlands	Thailand
California	India	New Zealand	Turkey
Canada	Indonesia	Norway	UAE
Chile	Iran	Pakistan	Ukraine
China	Ireland	Philippines	USA
Costa Rica	Israel	Portugal	USA—The South
Cuba	Italy	Saudi Arabia	Venezuela
Czech Republic	Japan	Scotland	Vietnam
Denmark	Korea	Singapore	

Barcelona At Your Door	Paris At Your Door	A Student's Guide
Beijing At Your Door	Rome At Your Door	A Traveller's Medical
Chicago At Your Door	San Francisco At	Guide
Havana At Your Door	Your Door	A Wife's Guide
Jakarta At Your Door	Shanghai At Your Door	Living and Working
Kuala Lumpur, Malaysia	Tokyo At Your Door	Abroad
At Your Door	Vancouver At Your Door	Personal Protection At
London At Your Door		Home & Abroad
Moscow At Your Door	A Globe-Trotter's Guide	Working Holidays
Munich At Your Door	A Parent's Guide	Abroad
New York At Your Door		

Illustrations by Han-dong Lee
Photographs from Korea National Tourism Corporation and Sonja Vegdahl

© 1988 Times Editions Pte Ltd
© 2000 Times Media Private Limited
© 2004 Marshall Cavendish International (Asia) Pte Ltd
Revised 1993, 1999, 2001, 2003
Reprinted 1994, 1995, 1996, 1997, 1998, 1999, 2000, 2001, 2004

This book is published by special
arrangement with Marshall Cavendish International (Asia) Pte Ltd
Times Centre, 1 New Industrial Road, Singapore 536196
International Standard Book Number 1-55868-621-5
Library of Congress Catalog Number 92-81940
Graphic Arts Center Publishing Company
P.O. Box 10306 • Portland, Oregon 97296-0306 • (503) 226-2402

Printed in Singapore

To our sons,
Anders and Erik

CONTENTS

PREFACE

Many of your encounters in Korea will be interesting, fun, thought-provoking, humorous, surprising and educational. Many more will be confusing, infuriating, shocking, anger-provoking and embarrassing. The expatriate who has adapted to living in Korea feels fortunate to live in this small, mountainous country; the newcomer often feels the frustrations of culture shock.

The majority of people who have made the 'land of the morning calm' their home for any period of time, find that it is a land with many things to love: the closeness with nature reflected in the architecture, designed foremost to harmonise with the natural surroundings; the national parks and the abundance of flowers and trees lining streets of crowded cities; the warmth and friendliness of the people that can be felt as soon as one sets foot on the land 42.5 million call home; the evidence of history and tradition blending comfortably with modern ways and more convenient structures. Many aspects of Korea are naturally attractive.

But even the most pleasant country can become a miserable place to live in when one does not know how to find the toilet, buy a bottle of shampoo, or catch a taxi. It is not even so much that things are different, for most newcomers are able to accept different values, customs and patterns of behaviour in other people, and eventually learn to go about their lives in a different way. The most difficult aspect of being transplanted into a new culture is that it seems impossible to comprehend. There seem to be so many dichotomies that cannot be understood from Western perceptions. Then, as soon as you think you are about to understand this ancient culture, some-thing happens to contradict what you thought you had figured out.

We hope in this book to help you understand Korea, so that most of your encounters with this rich eastern culture will be satisfying. In learning, you will not only be preparing yourself for an easier adjustment to a colourful and unique culture, but you will be expanding your concept of how people of different nationalities think, feel, act and communicate.

A word or two of caution before you read this book. The first is that we write from just one perspective. Our experiences and those of people we met in Korea may not ring true to others. The second is that Korea is changing at an unbelievable pace. Ever since the 1988 Olympics in Seoul, noticeable changes have become evident throughout the country – less alcohol consumption, a shift towards the nuclear family and the mushrooming of Western franchise restaurants, for example. Each region, family and individual changes in its own way, at its own speed. What is described in this book are general attitudes, patterns of behaviour and customs that many Koreans exhibit today. Certainly, there will be Koreans who do not fit these descriptions.

Having said that, we can also say that there are few people, Korean or non-Korean, who can claim to be familiar with every scrap of information in this book. In the course of our research, we were constantly surprised at how little we ourselves knew about a culture we had lived in for many years. And even more at how little many Koreans of this generation knew about their own customs.

We hope you will find pleasure in reading our book, just as we enjoyed writing it.

Sonja Vegdahl
Ben Seunghwa Hur
USA, 2003

ACKNOWLEDGEMENTS

Writing this book was anything but easy and would have been impossible without the help of many people. We would like to thank our parents who instilled in us an interest in and acceptance of people from other cultures. Throughout the writing of this book, they gave the kind of encouragement and support only they could have given.

We would also like to thank our students, Korean and non-Korean, who gave us general and specific insights into many of the topics covered in the book. Many of you do not know how much you stimulated us, as we were 'teaching' you.

We would like to thank a few organisations that offered generous assistance: FOCUS (Foreigners Community Service), the American Women's Club and the Royal Asiatic Society were particularly helpful in supplying vital information.

To many others living here in Korea, too numerous to mention, who spent untold hours carefully reading what we had written, giving helpful advice on the content, our sincere thanks. Hundreds of errors have been avoided through your careful scrutiny. Your enthusiasm about this book kept us going during the times the task seemed beyond us. You can be sure your questions and experiences will benefit others. As we would say in Korean, 'Kamsa-hamnida'.

8

– Chapter One –

LAND OF THE MORNING CALM

The Korean peninsula is mountainous, broken by narrow valleys, numerous small streams, long rivers and flat, fertile plains. Its total land area of 221,370 square kilometres (about the size of New Zealand) is bounded by China, the former USSR and Japan.

Korea is a 'tilted' country, with the higher regions in the northeast, and the lower in the southwest. The mountain range on the eastern coast is rugged, at places appearing higher than in reality. Few peaks on the peninsula exceed 1200 metres. These rocky eastern mountains meet the ocean abruptly, making the eastern coast a very scenic one. The western and southern coasts are extremely irregular, with some 3400 islands, the most famous being Cheju Island.

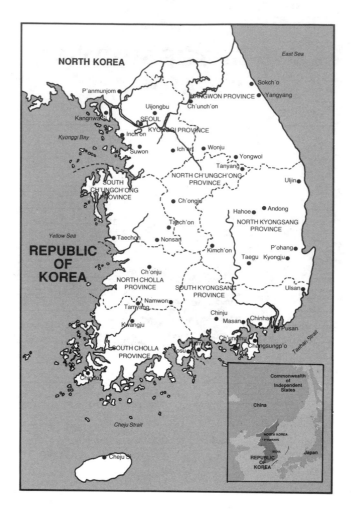

Much of Korea's cultivated land (20% of the total area) is in the south. Minerals, on the other hand, are more abundant in North Korea. North and South Korea are artificially divided by a 2000-kilometre demilitarised zone, at roughly the 38th parallel.

The population of the Republic of Korea, in the south, is about 45.2 million, making it one of the most densely populated countries in the world, denser than both India and Japan. North Korea is far less crowded, with a population about half as large as that of the Republic of Korea.

THE PEOPLE

Archaeologists believe that tribes from the Altai mountains began migrating to Manchuria and Siberia around 4000 BC. Some of them continued on to what is now the Korean peninsula, and settled there. (It is interesting to note that some of these people travelled further to Japan.)

The tribes that settled on the Korean peninsula eventually formed three kingdoms, which were first united in AD 668 under the Shilla dynasty. The Koreans share distinct physical characteristics, the same culture and one language, all of which have helped them retain their own identity, despite thousands of years of foreign invasions and several prolonged periods of non-Korean rule. Koreans today are deservedly proud of their old, enduring and unique culture, and of the race that they call their own.

It is difficult to attribute traits to a nation's people, as there are often almost as many exceptions to any rule as there are conformers. But newcomers to Korea and long-term residents alike do notice some particular 'Korean' characteristics and these are worthy of elaboration.

Endurance

The Korean people seem able to endure almost anything. They are extremely patient, waiting for their lot to improve, if not in this generation, perhaps in the next. No hardship seems too great to bear, including the attempt by Japan to 'ameliorate' the culture for 36 years, and the Korean War which destroyed much of the country and eventually resulted in its division.

Some of Korea's children on a school field trip. Exposure to the Korean heritage begins at an early age.

Similarly, individual Koreans seem able to withstand all kinds of hardships, be it from their rulers, teachers, employers or spouses! At times such endurance takes on a Buddhist-like fatalism, a feeling that the situation will never improve; at other times there seems to be an expectation that such long endurance will finally produce a reward.

Industry

Korean businessmen and housewives seem able to make something out of nothing. No effort is spared to accomplish a goal. Korea has very few natural resources, and it considers its biggest asset to be its highly educated people. South Korea's economic success is testimony enough to the industriousness of its people.

Emotion

Within their Confucian framework (see page 24), emotions must be discreetly controlled and rarely shown. But lurking behind the sometimes stoic Korean façade is a multitude of emotions. In certain situations, when these emotions can no longer be controlled, they may erupt into a passionate outburst. Koreans are especially sensitive to their own and other people's feelings, and such emotions play a big role in everyday behaviour. Positive emotions are strongly felt and expressed as warmth, loyalty and compassion.

Sense of Humour

Although Koreans are diligent, controlled and patient, they also possess a striking sense of humour. It is this characteristic that has enabled them to persevere under difficult circumstances.

Korean humour is evident in folk art, masked dances, puppet shows and even shamanistic exorcisms. Almost any gathering of Koreans seems to include at least one person with a special ability to make others laugh. Unfortunately for the foreigner, Korean wit rarely retains its humour when translated.

THE LANGUAGE

The Korean language is a member of the Altaic family and shares similarities with the Mongolian and Manchurian languages. Linguists also point out grammatical similarities between Korean, Finnish and Japanese, with the verb being always placed at the end of the sentence.

Although some Chinese words have been adopted into Korean, and Chinese characters are still used today, there are no similarities between Korean and Chinese grammar. Initially, Chinese characters were used by scholars in Korea, but in 1446 King Sejong invented *hangul,* the Korean alphabet, so that all Koreans could learn to read.

Hangul is a simple, scientific and phonetic alphabet consisting of 10 vowels, 11 vowel blends and 14 consonants which form syllables.

HANGUL

CONSONANTS

Letter	Pronunciation	Letter	Pronunciation
ㄱ	g	ㅇ	ng
ㄴ	n	ㅈ	j
ㄷ	d	ㅊ	ch
ㄹ	r	ㅋ	k
ㅁ	m	ㅌ	t
ㅂ	b	ㅍ	p
ㅅ	s	ㅎ	h

VOWELS

Letter	Pronunciation
ㅏ	ah
ㅑ	ya
ㅓ	o (as in dog)
ㅕ	yaw
ㅗ	oh
ㅛ	yo (as in yo-yo)
ㅜ	u (as in blue)
ㅠ	you
ㅡ	oo (as in good)
ㅣ	ee (as in see)
ㅐ	a (as in mat)

VOWEL BLENDS

Letter	Pronunciation
ㅒ	a (as in mat)
ㅖ	ye (as in yeah)
ㅔ	aye
ㅖ	ye (as in yellow)
ㅢ	way
ㅘ	wa (as in water)
ㅝ	wo (as in won)
ㅙ	wea (as in weather)
ㅞ	wei (as in weight)
ㅟ	wee
ㅢ	eui

Examples of syllables with vertical vowels (first consonant is placed to the left of the vowel, the last below the vowel):

Hangul	Pronunciation	Meaning
밤	bahm	night
말	mahl	horse
선	sun	line

Examples of syllables with horizontal vowels (first consonant is placed above the vowel, the last below the vowel):

Hangul	Pronunciation	Meaning
눈	noon	eye
문	moon	door
불	bool	fire

14

Compared to most alphabets, and especially to Chinese characters which take years to master, *hangul* is readily learned. The *hangul* alphabet is the one that remains in use in Korea today.

English can often be heard sprinkled within Korean conversation – words such as 'computer', 'supermarket', 'aspirin' and 'bus'. Many new and/or scientific foreign terms have been adopted. There is no hostility to employing such foreign words, and there even seems to be some special status associated with these words. Many products advertised on Korean television have English product names.

One can find several different romanisations of Korean words making place names especially problematic. Chamsil, Chamshil and Jamshil all refer to the same place. The problem is that the official roman spelling has changed over the years. Keep in mind that the romanisations ch and j, b and p, d and t, and s and sh are often used interchangeably.

HISTORY

Korean children study history throughout their 12 school years. It probably takes that long just to get a basic understanding of Korea's 5000 years of history. What follows is a shockingly brief summary, but it should help the foreigner understand more about Korean culture.

Much of Korea's history, up to the present day, has been influenced by its geography. The location of the Korean peninsula has made Korea particularly valuable for more powerful countries.

Beginnings

According to Korean legend, a heavenly king, Hwanin, sent his son, Hwanung, to earth. There he married a bear-turned-woman. They had a son, Tan-gun, the founder of the Korean race. Koreans celebrate Tan-gun's birthday as a national holiday, on 3 October, called Kae Chun Chul, literally 'sky opening day'.

15

The Three Kingdoms (c. 37 BC–AD 668)

Chinese records date the founding of Korea at 1122 BC. There are few records of Korean history until the time of the Three Kingdoms. The Koguryo kingdom was in the north, the first to emerge as a major power, and the first also to adopt Buddhism. The Paekche kingdom in the southwest developed next, and became known for its artistic creations. Finally, the Shilla kingdom came into being, emphasising military strength. These three kingdoms co-existed until 668, when the Shilla kingdom conquered the other two and unified the Korean peninsula.

The Unified Shilla Period (668–935)

The Shilla period ushered in great artistic accomplishments. Buddhism became the state religion, and even peasants subscribed to a simple form of Buddhism. The capital was located in Kyongju, a famous tourist spot today. As time passed, the economic disparity between the rulers and the ruled increased. Some of the leaders became corrupt, and internal power struggles among the leaders finally brought about the downfall of the government.

The Koryo Dynasty (935–1392)

The new dynasty, which lasted 400 years, was founded by Wang Kun. The Confucian system of government examinations for choosing civil servants by merit was adopted. The well-educated civil servants could censure royal decisions. Exquisite Koryo celadons were created during this period, and literature flourished. In 1238, the Mongols, who had taken control of China, swept over the Korean peninsula, destroying many Buddhist temples and works of art.

Internal problems also existed. Buddhist and Confucian scholars, who had co-existed peacefully until this time, came into conflict. Advocates of Confucianism, which had now reached Koryo, criticised the lavish spending on temples and opposed the custom of monks leaving their families, as this conflicted with the strong

One of the many reminders of Korea's history, this pagoda is part of Kyongbokkung Palace, built in 1392, which is located in downtown Seoul.

Confucian emphasis on filial piety. Yet another problem were the Japanese invasions. Previously on a small scale, by the mid-thirteenth century Japan had become an organised military power.

When the Mings took the Chinese throne from the Mongols, they disposed of the Koryo king who had supported the Mongols against them. This gave General Yi Song-gye an opportunity to seize the Koryo throne.

The Yi Dynasty (1392–1910)

The first Yi king moved the capital to Seoul, then called Hanyang *(Han* for river, *Yang* for the life-giving force). Castles were constructed there, and walls were built around the city.

To combat the corruption of the former Koryo government, and to give his own government legitimacy, the new ruler's first priority was to establish Confucianism. The anti-Buddhist movement of the late Koryo period continued, targeting Buddhism as the source of corruption and moral laxity. Strict Confucian rules, such as the separation of men and women, were put into practice, especially among the *yangban* (upper) class.

King Sejong

King Sejong ruled from 1418 to 1450 and is considered one of the greatest rulers in Korean history. His accomplishments were many and varied. Advances were made in the study of history, political studies, medicine and Confucian studies. Sundials, water clocks and rain gauges were invented. Agricultural information was compiled and distributed to the peasants.

King Sejong is best known for the creation of *hangul,* the Korean alphabet (see pages 13–15). Until then, only scholars were able to read, since mastering the Chinese characters used took years of concentrated study.

Foreign Invasion

In the late 1500s, the Japanese navy invaded the southern coast of Korea repeatedly with increasing power. The Koreans fought bravely, but had little chance against the numerically superior Japanese. Admiral Yi Sun Shin is known for his strong turtle boats which defeated the Japanese many times, but he, too, was finally killed in battle.

The fighting stopped when the Japanese emperor, Hideyoshi, died in 1598, but many towns along the Korean coast had been badly damaged. (At that time the Japanese captured some skilled makers of ceramics, who later helped develop the craft in Japan.)

The Hermit Kingdom

While Korea always maintained relations with China and Japan, it became increasingly wary of opening its doors to the West. It was afraid Western ideas would undermine the strong influence of Confucianism. Missionaries to Korea, while managing to convert some people, were sometimes killed. Missions from other countries were rejected and Korea's isolationist policies branded it the 'Hermit Kingdom'.

The Japanese Annexation (1909–1945)

While Korea was trying hard to keep out foreign influences, Russia, China and Japan were engaged in a power struggle to occupy Mongolia and Korea. After Japan had defeated China in 1895 and Russia in 1905, it forced Korea to accept the 'Protectorate Treaty' which regulated Japan's control over Korea's administrative and foreign relations functions. This treaty had the support of the United States and Britain. Although Korean uprisings to protest against this move were numerous and brave, Japan's military power was able to suppress the resistance, and eventually Japan annexed Korea. Japan controlled all aspects of Korean life – communication, transport, fisheries, timber, mining and land ownership. Children were educated in the Japanese language, and Koreans were forced to give up their names and adopt Japanese ones. Studying Korean history was illegal. Many Koreans were taken to Japan to work and serve in the Japanese army.

The Beginning of The Republic of Korea

When Japan surrendered at the end of World War II, the United States and the USSR agreed that the Korean land south of the 38th parallel would be temporarily administered by the United States.

The area north of the 38th parallel was to be administered by the USSR. But later, the two Korean regions were unable to reach an agreement on a unification formula. In 1948 Syngman Rhee was elected president of the south and Kim Il-Sung took power in the north.

The Korean War (1950–53)

In 1949, the United States withdrew its troops from Korea. The USSR also removed its troops, but left a well-trained and well-equipped North Korean military force. In June 1950, North Korea invaded its southern counterpart. Seoul was taken in three days, and within a month, the whole peninsula was controlled by the North except for the town of Pusan on the south coast.

The United States and other United Nations members sent reinforcements and pushed back the North Korean troops. But communist Chinese troops arrived to aid the North, forcing the UN troops to retreat. The UN forces gathered up strength, and again pushed the Northern troops back to roughly the area of the 38th parallel.

In July 1951, armistice talks began between the two halves, but a treaty was only signed two years later. It was only a temporary ceasefire agreement, and subsequent attempts for a more permanent agreement have all failed. The demilitarised zone remains unchanged.

The Korean War left the country in ruins. Thousands of families experienced the death of a family member. Thousands of orphans were left. Families were separated by the division of North and South. The economy and agricultural base suffered near total destruction.

Postwar Developments in South Korea

Syngman Rhee served as president of South Korea until he was forced to resign in April 1960. Chang Myon was elected prime minister in June 1960. Chang's government was unable to deal with the massive problems facing Korea, and a bloodless military coup overthrew it in May 1961.

Park Chung Hee, then a general, took over the government. Later, he resigned from the military and was elected as a civilian president. During the Third Republic, which lasted 17 years, unparalleled economic development was achieved.

In October 1979, Park was assassinated. Choi Kyu-hah was president for a short spell. He declared martial law but massive demonstrations continued. In December 1979, General Chun Doo Hwan took control of the government. He was indirectly elected in March 1981 for a single 7-year term.

In December 1987 the first direct presidential election was held. While charges of fraud were made, Roh Tae Woo, a former military academy classmate of Chun Doo Hwan, became the seventh president of the Republic of Korea. The Republic of Korea and North Korea were both admitted to the United Nations in October 1991, thus realising a long-held dream for many Koreans.

In 1992, Kim Young Sam defeated his long-term opposition party rival, Kim Dae Jung, in a presidential election. President Kim Young Sam began his administration by attacking bribery and corruption in the government. This led to the discovery that former presidents, Chun Do Hwan and Roh Tae Wooh, had both illegally garnered significant wealth during their presidencies. Chun was also convicted for his pivotal role and later cover-up in what is termed the "Kwangju Massacre". Later, Kim Young Sam and his family were also found to be involved in illegal, wealth-generating activities.

In an interesting turnaround, Kim Dae Jung, long considered too radical for most Koreans, was elected president in 1997. He took office just as the Asian economic crisis was beginning to have a serious and severe impact throughout Korea. The International Monetary Fund set up a strict plan to pull Korea out of serious financial problems. Today, people in Korea refer to their economy and lives as "before IMF" or "after IMF", so widespread were its consequences. Fortunately, Koreans responded to the crisis with their usual hard work and perseverance.

In 2002 Korea was the proud co-host of the 2002 FIFA World Cup. The event marked the first time that the World Cup had been held in Asia. The 64 tournament soccer games were divided equally between Korean and nearby Japan. Koreans used this opportunity to showcase their beautiful country and to demonstrate their warm hospitality.

Fortunately, under Kim Dae Jung's tenure, the economy rebounded, with Korea's estimated 2002 GDP growth rate at 6.2%. Korea's economic recovery after the Asian crisis surpassed that of her Asian neighbours. Economists are guardedly optimistic as they look at Korea's future economic growth despite the many uncertainties.

One of the most uncertain conditions is the tension created as a result from North Korea pulling out from an international nuclear arms treaty agreement. The United States president, after labelling North Korea an "Axis of Evil" country, was unwilling to continue further negotiations with North Korea until all nuclear development activities were halted. Amidst this climate of political instability, Roh Moo-hyun was elected president of South Korea.

President Roh, who took office in February 2003, ran on the Millennium Democratic Party, the party of former president Kim Dae Jung. President Roh has long been a champion of the poor and was a human rights lawyer, which resulted in his imprisonment. In his presidential campaign Roh made it clear that he would continue former president Kim Dae Jung's reunification policy (a policy that resulted in Kim being awarded the Novel Peace Prize in 2000). Unlike his rival presidential candidate, who supported the U.S. policy of cutting off contact with North Korea unless nuclear development was abandoned, President Roh believes that maintaining a dialogue with North Korea is vital, regardless of the actions North Korea may take.

Chapter Two

THE KOREAN WAY OF SEEING

'Going Dutch' is an efficient, fair way of paying for meals — to the Westerner. It is a selfish and unfriendly custom to the Korean. A hill to someone residing near the Alps might be a mountain to Koreans, who have few peaks over 1200 metres.

The perspective one uses for understanding events, for judging another's behaviour, or for deciding one's own behaviour, is largely defined by one's cultural background. It is a perspective learned from the earliest days of life and these lessons are reinforced by similar patterns of behaviour we observe in our own societies.

When one enters a new society, however, these old ways of perceiving may not work as well. For instance, many newcomers to

Korea assume that someone smiles because he finds something funny, or because he is happy. So when a secretary smiles after she has been blamed for forgetting to relay a message, the expatriate cannot understand the response. If he knew that a smile often means embarrassment or shame in Korea, the incident would make much more sense.

We cannot explain every particular aspect of Korean perception, but by looking at the basic ideas that influence Korean behaviour, we can begin to make some sense out of what we feel, see and hear. Confucianism plays a strong role and so does religion, which includes the 5000-year history of native shamanism. Family structure plays its part. And finally, the concepts of *kibun* and *nunchi* (see below) are two important manifestations of mood and feeling that have great bearing on most social interactions in Korea. We will also take a close look at the Korean view of strangers and acquaintances, and at Korean communication without words.

CONFUCIANISM

Perhaps nothing has shaped Korean society as much as Confucianism. In fact, many believe that Korea was influenced more by Confucianism than Confucius' native country, China.

Confucius, or K'ung Ch'iu, was a teacher and philosopher born in China in 551 BC. He believed leaders should be highly educated, that government should be in the hands of the most capable people rather than controlled by nobles, that everyone in society had a role, and if that role was carried out correctly, society would be just and good.

Confucius' teachings about the social structure of society and his system of education were first introduced to Korea during the Three Kingdoms (37 BC–AD 668). But they gained popularity only during the Yi dynasty (AD 1392–1910), when Buddhism was blamed for social corruption and Confucianism was upheld as a way to restore social order.

Confucian Ideals for Social Conduct

In Korea, Confucianism became a strict set of rules for social conduct, the effects of which can clearly be seen today.

Confucianism stressed the harmony of social relationships. Emotions were to be suppressed, and everyone was to follow the correct social order, so as not to disrupt the flow of society. The five most important relationships were specified, and the proper attitude governing these relationships was delineated:

- between father and son   –   filial piety
- between ruler and subject   –   loyalty
- between husband and wife   –   distinction in position
- between elder and younger   –   respect
- between friends   –   trust

Of these five, only the last one was a horizontal or equal relationship. The position of a person became as important as, if not more important than, who the person was. Korean social relationships today are still, by and large, vertical. Each person knows his position in relation to other people, and acts accordingly.

Ko Bong-seok, inside Kyongbokkung Palace in Seoul, an old hall where Confucian ceremonies of the Yi dynasty were held.

25

Family

The family is the basis of society. The leader of the country is the 'father' of his people and is ultimately responsible for their welfare. They, in turn, owe him their respect. Within a family unit, the father is responsible for the care of his family. If a family member violates a law, the father is accountable, as he should have raised that person to respect the law.

On page 39 we discuss the Korean family in greater detail.

Government

Selflessness and moral purity are necessary Confucian qualities for responsible, ethical leaders. People believed they had a right to expect such leaders, and also the right, moreover, to monitor their actions. An annual government examination, covering a diverse range of subjects, was used to select leaders.

During the Yi dynasty in Korea, only people of the high *yangban* class were eligible to take this examination. Though Korea has not often had such noble leaders, most Koreans today still judge government leaders at all levels by these high Confucian moral standards. A corrupt government officer, once discovered, is expected to be quickly relieved of his post.

Education

Confucianism's stress on the importance of education has influenced all Asian countries. Even second and third generation Asians in Western countries tend to perform better than their non-Asian counterparts.

The value of education is similarly deeply impressed upon Koreans. Education is seen as the only path to success, as well as a valuable pursuit in and of itself. Until recently, a professor occupied the highest position in Korean society. Teachers at all levels are owed a lifelong reverence by grateful and respectful students.

Roles of Men and Women

While few question the positive effects in Korea of Confucian respect for elders and education, many criticise the effect Confucianism has had on the lives of Korean women.

During the Unified Shilla period (668–935), women enjoyed nearly equal legal status with men. But in the latter part of the Koryo dynasty (935–1392) and even more in the Yi dynasty that followed, Confucianism dictated inequality for women. Boys and girls were permanently separated after the age of five. Sons of the high or *yangban* class received an education in Confucian classics, and later were eligible to compete for the government examination. Girls remained with their mothers, learning housecraft until they were married, and controlled by their mothers-in-law as soon as they were married.

A woman could not commit these seven evils (*chilgo chiak*):

- Disobeying her in-laws
- Bearing no son
- Committing adultery
- Jealousy
- Carrying a hereditary disease
- Excessive chatter
- Larceny

The husband or parents-in-law of a transgressor had the right to turn her out. She was, moreover, forbidden to return to her own parents' home. No matter what their husbands did, however, women could not divorce them.

During the Yi dynasty, women were not supposed to be seen by non-family members. They remained confined at home. In the evening, a bell would ring, warning men off the streets so that women could go out briefly. Some were less fortunate: one older Korean woman recalls being thrilled when her family escaped to Pusan during the Korean War, as it was her first glimpse beyond the walls of her home.

The Confucian emphasis on education can be seen today, as vast numbers of students compete for places in the top universities of Korea.

While Korean women today are not imprisoned, their lives are relatively restricted. This is one aspect of living in Korea that surprises expatriates the most. A man and a woman may study in the same university engineering department, and may be hired by the same company. But while the man would get an engineering job, the woman would be more likely to be employed making coffee and wiping the desks of her male colleagues. Companies would generally choose to hire a less qualified man over a woman, presumably because they would expect a woman's family responsibilities would interfere with her job.

Boy babies are still strongly preferred to girls, because boys remain part of the family, whereas girls are only temporary members who leave their parents when they marry. Men support their parents in their old age; women serve their parents-in-law.

Women have no legal rights over their children, who belong to their fathers and their fathers' relatives. If a couple divorces, custody of the children almost always goes to the father.

Marriage Law

Rulers of the Yi dynasty were strict about intra-family marriage. Family records exist today that have been kept for more than 500 years and specify one's paternal ancestor. Any two people coming from the same paternal ancestor (even though it was 500 years ago) may not marry. This has caused great anguish to some modern-day couples.

This rule is particularly strange as it assumes that all of a person's genes came from the father. Maternal relatives can marry after the fourth generation.

RELIGION

Like many other aspects of Korean life, religion is a mixture of beliefs introduced by people from other countries, and modified to fit Koreans.

The earliest religion was a form of animism, paying tribute to the ten thousand spirits of nature. Buddhism entered Korea during the period of the Three Kingdoms (37 BC–AD 668). Confucianism, which served the function of religion, predominated during the Yi dynasty. Christianity was first introduced during the Japanese invasions in 1592, but did not gain a foothold in Korea until much later (see below, page 32).

Though a large number of Koreans do not claim allegiance to any of the major religions, they are influenced by Confucianism and Buddhism, while shamanism is certainly alive and well in many Korean homes.

Buddhist monks pray to enter the nirvana circle around the Tabot'ap Pagoda at the courtyard of Pulguksa Temple. This pagoda is considered a masterpiece of stone sculpture surviving from the Shilla period.

Buddhism

Buddhism probably has the largest following of any organised religion in Korea. According to some records, it was introduced, via China, to the northernmost kingdom, Koguryo, in AD 372, then spread to the other two kingdoms, becoming especially prominent during the Unified Shilla period (AD 668–935). At that time many Buddhist temples were built throughout Korea, and monks were revered.

Buddhism continued to flourish during the Koryo dynasty (AD 935–1392). A treasured cultural relic of the Koryo dynasty and a significant landmark in the history of Buddhism are the 81,258 wooden printing plates of the ancient Buddhist scripture, the *Tripitoka*, carved between 1237 and 1252. (The first movable metal type was developed in Korea in 1377, some 200 years before Gutenberg.) After prominence in the Koryo dynasty, Buddhism lost the status it enjoyed when the Yi dynasty came into power in 1392. Buddhism was blamed for much social corruption and Buddhist monks were driven out of Seoul.

During the Japanese annexation, Buddhism became visible again as the Japanese promoted similarities between Korea and Japan. But only in recent years has Buddhism been able to regain some of its popularity. There are now more than 7 million avowed Buddhists, and perhaps twice that many practise the faith in some way or other. There are about 25,000 clergy of both sexes, and monks are seen throughout Korea in their grey robes and pointed straw hats. Koreans of all faiths appreciate the 7244 accredited temples scattered in picturesque locations throughout the country.

As Buddhism has been a presence for thousands of years, even non-Buddhist Koreans have absorbed some of its subtle aspects. For instance, because of their belief in Buddhist *karma,* Koreans have developed a fatalistic, accepting approach to their problems, as well as great patience in dealing with difficulties that they believe to be inevitable.

Note to Expats

Buddhist temples are common tourist destinations for Koreans and expatriates alike. A serene temple nestled against a mountain, surrounded by the fresh blooms of spring, flaming colours of autumn, or snow-topped hillsides, is a quick cure for the stress one feels from fast-paced city life. Buddhist temples are found throughout the country, in remote areas as well as in cities. Generally a number of buildings are located inside the stone wall which surrounds the temple area. Visitors are free to look around at will – taking photographs and talking quietly are not discouraged. The building which holds a statue of Buddha generally has several steps and an open sliding door at the top of the stairs. If one desires to go inside, shoes must be left in the area near the sliding doors. Buddhists then enter the room, bow once or several times towards the Buddha statue, and meditate for a while, sometimes putting incense on the altar. Others may enter this room as well, taking care to be quiet.

Christianity

Korea's first contact with Christianity was probably during the Japanese Hideyoshi invasions of 1592–98, when a Roman Catholic priest accompanied the Japanese General Konishi Yukinaga, a Catholic convert. The priest converted no Koreans, however.

In 1777, during the reign of King Chongjo, a young scholar, Yi Sung Hun, went to Beijing where he was introduced to Christianity by Jesuit missionaries, and was baptised. Upon his return, he converted many Koreans, including members of a prominent family, and the first Christian church was founded. Korean Catholics today take great pride in the fact that Christianity was introduced to the country by the laity, and not by missionaries.

At the end of the 18th century, there were about 4000 Christians, but practising Christianity in a strongly Confucian country was rather difficult. Christians often refused to perform ancestral ceremonies, which did not make them popular with the Confucian government. Persecution of the Catholic missionary movement drove it underground.

Protestantism made its first major inroad in 1884, when Dr Horace Allen came to Korea as a physician for foreign diplomatic officers. Later, as the royal family physician, he went on to found the first Western-style hospital. The Protestants had the advantage of entering Korea more than a century after the Catholics, learning from their failure. Moreover, they worked within the government system, focusing on providing health care and education.

During the Japanese occupation, both Protestantism and Catholicism gained popularity amongst Koreans. The Christian ideals of

Two shaman totem poles stand guard against evil spirits.

humanity, social mobility, equality and democracy were particularly attractive at that time.

After many Christians escaped from North Korea to the south during the Korean War, Korea's Christian churches grew remarkably. Today there are about 11 million Christians in Korea, roughly 25% of the total population, the second highest percentage of any East Asian country after the Philippines.

As with Buddhism, Christianity has left its mark on all Koreans. The Christians introduced the concept of education for women and equality of the sexes. Christian leaders in Korea today are actively vocal about social problems, and are highly respected.

Note to Expats

There is a wide variety of churches, synagogues and mosques with services available in several Western languages. Information about these is given in English-language newspapers every Saturday. Joining a familiar place of worship is an excellent way to ease oneself into an unfamiliar culture. Most international places of worship are particularly sensitive to the needs of expatriates, and their members provide support for one another.

Shamanism

Advocates of Buddhism, Confucianism and Christianity in Korea made some very strong attempts to eradicate shamanism, but none succeeded. Besides serving a religious function in the lives of Koreans, shamanism provides entertainment, not to mention psychological and social benefits.

So entrenched is the belief in spirits, that aspects of shamanism have been incorporated into the other religions. Observe, for example, that most Buddhist houses in Korea have a spirit house. Some Christian rituals, such as praying for long periods, were perhaps more readily accepted by Koreans because of the similarity of these acts to shamanistic traditions.

Doubtless in this same spirit of sharing, aspects of other religions have also been incorporated into shamanism. Some shamanistic spirits took on the image of Buddha when Buddhism spread across Korea. And when Confucianism stressed the need for women to bear sons, it suddenly became general knowledge that the Mountain Spirit had the ability to produce sons.

Perhaps shamanism exists today in Korea because of its ability to co-exist with the other religions. Shamanistic ceremonies are held when international companies open new multi-storeyed offices in Seoul. When Western medicine and traditional Korean medicine both fail to cure an illness, a shaman is summoned to perform a *kut* or exorcism (see page 36), in case evil spirits are the culprits.

Most Koreans participate in shamanistic rituals. For some, they are a source of entertainment; for some others they are a mere formality. For the rest, the spirits exist and must be appeased to prevent misfortune.

According to shamanism, spirits exist in every part of nature. Every river, mountain, animal and home has a spirit. Everyone who dies has one, that may or may not move on to another world. These spirits are not inherently good or bad, but if treated badly, they bring about misfortune, including sickness, natural disaster and family discord. When worshipped or summoned, however, they help prevent problems and ensure good luck.

Koreans are careful to summon the right spirit. For example, the Dragon King assists by providing bountiful rain, but has no power to cure an illness.

Mudangs

The *mudang* or Korean shaman, who is always a woman, has the special ability to communicate with spirits and is the go-between of the spirit world. There are records of *mudangs* from as early as the Shilla period, when, even then, they were women. *Mudangs* have played an important role in Korea's history as they were close to the rulers, advising on state affairs. During the Yi dynasty, despite government damping down of shamanistic practices, *mudangs* were still employed by the royal family. In fact, they were among the few women allowed to have contact with men.

Mudangs are thought to be 'called' by the spirits to serve that function. A woman, single or married, may have had a psychotic episode where she loses contact with people. The only way she can escape such episodes is by becoming a *mudang*. There are families of hereditary *mudangs* who earn a living visiting villages to perform annual or biannual ceremonies, the villagers' insurance of adequate rain, health and general prosperity.

With her special ability, one would have imagined that the *mudang* was revered, but this is not the case. On the contrary, she is considered to belong to one of the lowest social classes in Korea, even by those who consult her. Koreans would be ashamed to own up to having a *mudang* in the family.

Kuts

A *kut* is a shamanistic ceremony during which a *mudang* makes spiritual contact. Ceremonies range from the very simple (one *mudang*, a client and a few friends) to the dramatic (several *mudangs*, costumes, props and a large audience). Simple *kuts* last a few hours, large ones run to several days and great expense.

The purpose is to resolve a problem, usually serious, such as an illness or a downturn in business. A *kut* is especially important when a family member has died prematurely – unmarried or childless – for the spirits of such people are reluctant to move on to the next world. They remain tied to earth, creating problems for their living relatives. It is imperative, therefore, to persuade them, via the *mudang*, to travel smoothly to the next world.

At a larger *kut*, the *mudang* will wear various costumes symbolising the spirit she is trying to attract. A drummer beats out a rhythm, the *mudang* sings, chants and dances, at first slowly, then teasingly and violently, to attract a particular spirit. When the spirit arrives, he speaks through the *mudang*: a deceased relative may want to express some last thoughts; a living relative may wish to convey something; a dissatisfied spirit may make demands.

An important part of the *kut* is the drama. The bright colours, fans, knives and lanterns set the stage for the advent of spirits. It is lively entertainment for the audience who may even join in the dancing.

The *mudang's* performance must be convincing. She becomes not only a spirit medium, but an actress, dancer, magician, comedienne and musician. When speaking for the general spirit, she may balance on two razor-sharp knives with bare feet. During the *kut,* she may hold out her fan, asking the audience to donate coins to the greedy spirit. She may walk across a 'bridge' made only of paper, held high in the air by two assistants. The *mudang* may rip long white cloth with her body, symbolising the final separation between the deceased and the living.

Note to Expats

Many expatriates have enjoyed the drama of a *kut. Kuts* are sometimes advertised in the English-language newspapers. There are also particular places, usually in the mountains, where *kuts* are held for people who cannot have them at home. At special times of the year, shamanistic ceremonies are held to call upon the spirit of a river or mountain.

The presence of foreigners does not seem to disturb the atmosphere, but please be sensitive to the mood. Though some Koreans view a *kut* as merely a form of entertainment, to the participants it is a spiritual experience.

If possible, attend with a Korean friend who can explain rituals to you. Follow what the rest of the audience do. Bring some money (of small denomination) to donate to the spirits at particular points of the *kut*. You may well have a chance to sample some of the food and wine, after it has been offered to the spirits.

37

Kosas

These shamanistic ceremonies celebrate the opening of a new office or the construction of a new home, ship or aeroplane. In essence, spirits are asked to give their blessing to the new endeavour. *Kosas* are still held in Korea, even though many discredit their spiritual value. A pig's head, food and wine are set out on a table. Wine is poured over the ground or the particular object requiring the blessing, and the participants bow deeply. At a big *kosa*, a *mudang* may be invited to bring even more luck, and dancers are brought in to add to the celebration and ceremony.

Housewives, usually older Korean women, hold a *kosa* at home once or twice every year, to ask for the blessings of the house spirits. One of these is thought to reside in the roofbeam, another beside the chimney. There is no place for such spirits in high-rise apartments, so these rituals are becoming obsolete.

Fortune Telling

Their special connection with spirits makes *mudangs* expert at predicting fortunes. The blind are also believed to have a special ability to 'see' into the future.

Many Koreans today seek the advice of a fortune teller at particular times: mothers consult one before their children marry, to determine the compatibility of the new couple; parents confirm the suitability of a newborn baby's name; families require advice over the appropriateness of a burial site for a family member. Fortune tellers are especially busy before a university entrance examination and at the beginning of the year, when people need advice in planning the year's activities. It is very common for businessmen to consult fortune tellers before making important business decisions.

A Korean's fortune depends primarily on the year, month, day and time of birth, collectively known as *saju*. Twelve animals represent different years, months, days and times, and the combination of these animals is thought to determine one's future.

In Korea, visiting a psychologist is considered a sign of serious mental weakness, but it is perfectly acceptable to visit a fortune teller. In many ways, fortune tellers serve the function of mental health professionals. They are supportive and sympathetic towards their clients, and can reduce the guilt and responsibility suffered for unfortunate incidents. A deserted wife may be told, for example, that her present circumstances are her 'destiny', and quite beyond her control.

THE FAMILY

Of the five important relationships that Confucianism defines, three deal with the family: father/son, husband/wife, and elder brother/ younger brother. According to Confucianism and Korean tradition, the family is the basis for society. The Korean family (*kah jok*) is slowly changing, but these rules still dominate most family interactions today.

Besides being the basic element of Korean society, the Korean family is based on the male family line. An extremely important document, the family register includes the names of a Korean's paternal ancestors for over 500 years. The continuity of this bloodline is critical, and possible only by having sons. Ending a family line, by failing to produce sons, is considered unfilial, and must be avoided at all costs. In the recent past, men have married a second or third time in order to rectify such a disaster. Even today, many young couples are distressed when they have only daughters.

Male Dominance

The Korean family focuses on the male. A paternal grandmother is a 'real grandmother', whereas the maternal one is the 'outside grandmother'. The family bloodline, so important to Koreans, is only traced on the father's side. When a woman marries, she becomes a member of her husband's family. Her name is crossed off her father's family register and added to the husband's.

As male heirs are the only real family members, sons are clearly preferred over daughters. Traditionally, a Korean wife's primary duty was to bear sons for her husband's family. Unfortunately, even though she must legally and socially leave her own family, she is rarely considered a real family member in her husband's family, since her blood is not from that family.

Respect for Parents and Ancestors

As parents are responsible for their children's whole being and have sacrificed much to raise their children, Koreans have traditionally believed they owe their parents everything. While Westerners acknowledge their debt to their parents, Koreans feel a much deeper obligation, one that cannot be repaid in their parents' lifetimes or even after death.

Ancestral ceremonies are held in honour of deceased parents several times a year. They are performed for the three previous generations (parents, grandparents and great-grandparents). Ancestral ceremonies are performed only for one's paternal ancestors, and women generally do not participate.

Extended Family

Nuclear family living arrangements are increasingly common in Korea, but the concept of what a family is has changed very little.

A Korean family consists of grandparents, their sons, the sons' wives and the sons' children. If a family is fortunate to have four living generations, all are included in the family. Members of this family unit are intimately tied to each other, and one member's affairs are every member's concern. The oldest male relative has the final say in important matters, such as which university a family member should attend, whom he should marry, or what job he should accept. He is likely to consult other members before making a decision.

Other relatives on the father's side, such as great-uncles, their wives, second cousins and so on are also considered part of the family.

These more extended relatives participate in weddings and *hwangap* (60th birthday) celebrations, but other contact with them is not too frequent. Koreans have fewer responsibilities towards these more distant relatives.

The tie with maternal relatives is also important, particularly between mothers and daughters, and between siblings. Emotional and financial support is found in these relationships. When a woman is pregnant, she often lives with her mother. After childbirth, it is common for the maternal grandmother to help care for the baby. While the child's paternal grandparents are legally tied to him, many young couples find that social relationships are easier when the maternal grandparents babysit.

Care for the Elderly

Korea has no nationwide public insurance for the aged, but tradition has provided a secure, happy life for the elderly. The first son and his wife are responsible for taking care of the parents when they retire.

Often, when the first son marries, he and his bride live with his parents. The daughter-in-law has an obligation to obey her mother-in-law, learn the ways of the family, and care for the ageing parents until their deaths. In some families, personality conflicts or poverty may cause aged parents to be cared for by another son. When there are no sons, a daughter takes on the responsibility.

Family Roles

A clear hierarchy exists in the Korean family, and no two people are equal.

The patriarch occupies the highest position, his wife coming after him. The children are ranked by age. Even twins are unequal, the first-born requiring respect from his marginally younger sibling. When sons marry, their wives' status depends on their own positions. So, even if the second son's wife is older than the first son's wife, the former must show respect to the latter.

Hundreds of words are used to specify and address other family members. The father's older brother and father's younger brother are referred to by different words. And their wives are also addressed differently. Most young Koreans know only some of the forms of address.

Male Roles

The husband/father is sometimes referred to as the 'outside person'. His greatest responsibility is providing the family income. Traditionally, he has had greater responsibility towards his parents than to his wife or children, but this is slowly changing. His needs generally come before those of his wife and children, but not before those of his parents.

The eldest son is responsible for his parents when they grow older. If his father is no longer able to support the family, the eldest son must pay for the education and marriages of his younger siblings. Younger children in turn must show him respect, which may take the form of cleaning his room or running errands for him.

While boys are expected to show respect to older family members, they have few responsibilities in the home beyond occasionally looking after younger siblings and running errands.

Female Roles

The wife/mother is responsible for all 'inside' work. As the 'inside person', she devotes herself to raising her children and providing a comfortable home for her family. If she lives with her in-laws, she is obliged to serve them. There is a compensating factor. Women generally hold the purse-strings. After giving his entire salary to his wife, a man receives an allowance from her.

Traditionally, the relationship between a Korean man and his wife was not a close friendship. Rather, as the old Confucian doctrine prescribes, it was characterised by a distinction of roles. Recently, however, Korean women have begun to demand a more active role in society, working outside their homes. They also expect their husbands to participate in household affairs and desire a more romantic relationship with them. Korean men do not appear too eager to move away from the traditional, male-oriented society, and feminist reforms will certainly not sweep the country overnight. Nevertheless, women today see themselves as much more equal to men than did women ten years ago. Young married couples also tend to reject the traditional, hierarchical male-female relationship of their parents' generation.

Girls tend to have more family responsibilities than boys. As they grow older, they help their mothers with household chores, washing clothes, cooking and cleaning. They are also required to look after their younger siblings.

KIBUN

To understand Korean interpersonal relationships, behaviour and thought is to know the concept of *kibun*. Like other culture-laden words, there is no exact English equivalent. *Kibun* relates to mood, current feeling and state of mind. To hurt someone's *kibun* is to hurt his pride, to cause loss of dignity and to bring about loss of face.

Korean interpersonal relationships operate on the principle of harmony. Maintaining a peaceful, comfortable atmosphere is more important than attaining immediate goals or telling the absolute truth. Koreans believe that to accomplish something while causing unhappiness or discomfort to individuals is to accomplish nothing at all. If relationships are not kept harmonious, it is difficult, if not impossible, to work towards any goal. All cultures value how their members feel emotionally, but few cultures value this as much as Koreans do. To Koreans, to put greater emphasis on efficiency, honesty or some higher form of moral integrity, is to be cold and unfeeling.

Kibun enters into every aspect of Korean life. Knowing how to judge the state of other people's *kibun,* how to avoid hurting it, and keeping your own *kibun* in a satisfactory state are important skills.

Those who ignore the significance of *kibun* will find many

43

unnecessary obstacles in their paths. If you need something done, for example, but can see that the *kibun* of the person required to do it is not in a good state, it would be foolish to make the request. (The means by which one judges another's *kibun* is called *nunchi*. This is discussed below.)

To foreigners, Koreans seem overly sensitive and emotional, and their *kibun* seems to be hurt too easily. For example, a Korean's *kibun* is damaged when his subordinate does not show proper respect, that is, by not bowing soon enough, not using honorific words, not contacting the superior within an appropriate period of time, or worse, handing something to him with the left hand. Most of these rules of etiquette are well known to Koreans, and while they are often difficult or cumbersome to remember, they must be heeded to avoid hurting *kibun*.

Sometimes, even for Koreans, the rules are not clear and one can inadvertently damage someone's *kibun*. If you do not know the person's position in relation to yourself, and treat him as an inferior, his *kibun* will be hurt, and he may not wish to continue a relationship with you. Or, in ignorance of the fact, you may say something derogatory about his home town. You may even mistakenly believe an older classmate to be in the same 'class' and call him by name, rather than addressing him as *hyung* (older brother).

Bad news – a negative financial report or an employee's error, for example – is generally brought to an office at the end of the day, to give the recipient time to recover before the next day. And people are almost always fired without any notice, for who can continue working when their *kibun* has been so badly damaged? Giving a less expensive gift than the receiver would deem appropriate can also injure *kibun*.

As Korea is a hierarchical society, this sensitivity is most important with regard to people of a higher status. A superior often does not consider the feelings of those of lower status. But then inferiors have less face to lose! If a husband rebukes his wife in public, she is not nearly as humiliated, her *kibun* is not as damaged as her husband's would be in the reverse situation.

Note to Expats

When interacting socially with Koreans, it is essential to bear in mind the importance of *kibun*. As a foreigner, you will be forgiven some offences. But the more value you place on *kibun* as opposed to accomplishing material goals, the more respected you will be, and the better your relations with Koreans will be.

NUNCHI

Closely tied to *kibun* is another Korean concept, *nunchi,* which literally means 'eye measure'. It is the ability to assess another person's *kibun,* but it is done not only by the eye.

In a society where behaving so as not to disturb social harmony is critical, being able to judge another person's state of mind is essential. Good *nunchi* ability puts a person one step ahead of everyone else. He will know when to ask his boss for favour, when to take or yield the right of way in traffic, and when to tell bad news and cause the least damage.

Nunchi is a kind of antenna one has to sense another's feelings. Some of this is done by watching body language, heeding the tone of voice and what is said. In Korea, where *kibun* is so important, many people have developed a kind of sixth sense with which to assess it.

Of course, this kind of judgement takes place everywhere in the world, as when a child learns the best time and person to ask for an ice cream or treat. But whereas Westerners are more likely to state their moods, or at least reveal their states of mind, Koreans have been taught to control their emotions, and to disguise their true feelings. To discern the mood of a Korean requires much *nunchi.*

Some Koreans complain about the indirectness with which they are required to express their feelings. They would sometimes prefer to say exactly how they feel, and often wish others would do the same, thus negating the need for such a sensitive *nunchi.* But tradition dies hard in this Confucian-oriented society.

Note to Expats

It is impossible for people from different cultures to read one another's verbal and nonverbal messages accurately. Of course, the better you can do so, the better off you will be. Being aware of the sensitive way your own mood is being judged by others, particularly by people of lower status, may help you understand their behaviour.

Remember, too, that the temperature gauges of feelings in Korean and Western societies are different. Thus, an angry outburst may be taken as an expression of greater dissatisfaction in Korea than in a Western country. If you receive a phone call bearing bad news, and appear sad after it, your maid will probably tiptoe around all day, afraid to upset you further. If you complain to your maid about washing the dishes in cold water, she may misinterpret this to mean that you are generally dissatisfied with her work.

What is an insensitive expatriate to do? Be prepared for some misunderstandings, and realise that when they happen, both parties are equally to blame, as neither of you understands the other's culture quite well enough.

STRANGERS AND ACQUAINTANCES

One thing that puzzles new expatriates in Korea is how differently people are treated in different situations. The newly arrived foreign businessman will be shown extreme politeness and kindness, even though he is meeting business people for the first time. But later, as he tries to catch a taxi, he may be pushed aside, and even stepped on, without so much as a word of apology. The two types of behaviour contradict each other. Koreans are both extremely polite and extremely rude!

Strangers

In Western societies there are rules of etiquette for relating to strangers. These rules include such concepts as:

Neighbours work together to make ground red pepper, an essential spice in many Korean dishes.

- First come, first served
- Not intruding upon a stranger's physical space
- Helping anyone in particular need

In Korea, a person to whom one has not been introduced, with whom one has had no previous interactions, nor foresees any future relationship, is not considered a person. There are no rules to follow when relating to a 'non-person'.

Before you condemn Koreans for this seemingly barbaric behaviour, take a look at Korea's agricultural background and the tedious requirements of interacting with persons with whom a Korean had some relationship. Not so long ago, most Koreans lived in small agricultural villages. Everyone was connected to everyone else, including people they had never met. So everyone followed the strict

47

Korean rules of etiquette, even when dealing with strangers. Then people moved to large cities, where there were no particular connections with others. With little money, time or energy, and an abundance of people who had a claim on their resources, it was impossible for Koreans to treat everyone properly, in the old way. Perhaps the only way to avoid helping and giving respect to the hundreds of needy strangers on the street, was to pretend that they did not exist. To recognise their existence was to treat them generously and politely.

Another reason was the anonymity of cities: dishonest people could steal and cheat without being labelled for the rest of their lives. It became dangerous to trust others or to act kindly. Strangers came to be viewed as people 'out to get you', people who did not consider others worthy of respect.

Acquaintances

Most of the people a Korean has any regular contact with are considered worthy of proper treatment. Past and present neighbours, those who provide services, teachers (his or hers and those of people he or she knows), anyone who has attended the same schools – all of these automatically fit into this category.

People working in the same company, though never introduced, are also considered part of this sphere of human relationships. Friends and anyone a friend has introduced also deserve proper treatment.

In reality, there are hundreds, perhaps thousands of people in one's life who deserve proper treatment. These relationships require an enormous amount of time, money and psychological energy. It would seem almost impossible to treat all those people in the same way. Yet those hundreds of people connected to a Korean are treated with kindness, humbleness and due respect.

Note to Expats

In Korea, you will be treated very kindly by most of the Koreans you meet. Korea generally lives up to its reputation as the country of politeness. There will nevertheless be times when you will be treated as a 'non-person', and the experience of those occasions may stay with you for a long while.

Until rather recently, people in the homogenous Korean society had few chances to see foreigners, who are still somewhat novel to many Koreans. One Korean misconception is that non-Koreans cannot understand their language, so when they say something about a foreigner in his presence, they imagine he will not understand. As an expatriate in Korea, you may be pointed at, your clothes and hairstyle analysed, and your figure evaluated, all in your presence. As one expatriate commented, it is as though you were a character on television, unaware of the attention and therefore undisturbed by it.

Some expatriates have gone so far as to say that Koreans consider all foreigners 'non-persons'. This is perhaps too extreme. A Korean who has a relationship with an expatriate treats him with all the politeness that only 'real' persons deserve. In fact, except for talking about them in their presence, Koreans show more politeness to expatriates, even those they do not know, than they do to other Koreans. Sometimes that extra politeness may not always seem polite enough, but luckily, most of your time will be spent with people who do consider you a 'real' person, and who treat you with much more kindness than you would expect in your home country.

NONVERBAL COMMUNICATION

Although some nonverbal behaviour is universal (crying, frowning, laughing and blushing, for example), much of it is unique to its culture. Nonverbal communication can support, emphasise or contradict what one says verbally. Many expatriates in Korea find that much communication that would be stated verbally in their own countries is communicated nonverbally in Korea.

For example, when one is riding a bus with a heavy load of books, and there is no seat, it is common for a seated person to offer to hold the books. The offer includes no verbal sound. The seated person merely tugs at the books until the holder realises he is not trying to steal them, but is actually offering to hold them. At first, many expatriates think Koreans communicate nonverbally because they assume the foreigner knows no Korean. If you observe Koreans in the same situation, however, you will notice that they communicate with each other nonverbally as well. For Koreans, it is awkward to talk to someone who has not been introduced, and this nonverbal communication is comfortable for all concerned.

Some other examples of nonverbal communication are described below.

Bowing

One of the first things visitors to Korea notice is the bowing. The bow can symbolise many things, and is performed by each person many times a day.

When one Korean meets another for the first time in a day, it is appropriate to bow and say *'Annyŏng haseyo'*. The person of lower status should bow and say this first, and the other should respond quickly with the same bow and greeting. If the other person has a much greater status, such as that between father and child, he does not bow, but uses intimate language in the greeting. You can guess the relative status of two people by the way they greet each other. A teacher and his student, an employer and his employee, an uncle and his niece are all easily distinguished by their bows.

A Korean bows when introduced to someone for the first time. The introducer briefly presents the two people to each other; one of them bows and softly says his own name, and the other responds in the same manner. Name cards are then exchanged, face up, since it is difficult to hear the names, and this will give each person more information about the other, as well as his position.

Koreans bow when they part. This time they say (to the one leaving) *'Annyŏnghi gaseyo'* and (to the one staying) *'Annyŏnghi gyeseyo.'* Translated, these mean 'Go (or stay) in peace.' Koreans are all familiar with the English 'goodbye' and tend to use it when speaking to expatriates.

Some more unique forms of bowing are reserved for special occasions, particularly when one wants to show an unusual degree of respect. In the most respectful kind, the Korean lowers his or her head all the way to the ground, and touches both palms to the floor. This is done after a marriage ceremony, at ancestors' graves and during the New Year celebrations.

Note to Expats

Learning to bow is like learning a language – if it is not done before one reaches adolescence, it can never be done perfectly. Practice does not seem to help. Expatriates always look a little strange bowing.

Bowing in the right circumstances, however, no matter how clumsily, will win points with Koreans. It shows that you are trying (no matter if unsuccessfully) to fit into their culture. Actually, even for a foreigner, bowing seems to be the natural thing to do in response to another's bow. Some expatriates who spend most of their time around Koreans even find themselves bowing to other Westerners!

Personal Space

Personal space is a rare commodity in Korea. This is natural in a country with one of the highest population densities in the world. Koreans are used to sleeping, working, eating and standing in conditions that would be considered far too crowded by many Westerners. Even in smaller towns throughout Korea, pavements are so narrow that, no matter how few people walk on them, they will manage to bump into each other. The imaginary bubble of air that many expatriates like having around them will certainly be intruded upon constantly in Korea.

This invasion of personal space can be one of the more irritating aspects of living in Korea for some expatriates. Walking on the street, standing in a lift, working with other people in an office, or visiting

Space is at a premium in Seoul. The Western taboo regarding the invasion of personal space is not always observed by Koreans.

the local market can all become affronts to one's personal space. You are often not aware of the stress caused by such encounters, but it is there, nonetheless. Even in one's home, the maid may decide to wash the dishes as the expatriate housewife is putting together a meal, even if this means the elbows of both will be colliding every three seconds. This does not bother most Koreans, so they do not think about it.

Worse than the constant bumping, tripping and colliding are the seemingly deliberate attempts to cross paths with strangers on the street. On a street wide enough for four people, two crossing will more often than not manage to brush past each other. When an expatriate is regularly subjected to such behaviour, it can overshadow all of the positive interactions he has had with Koreans. 'Why,' he asks, 'did that Korean intentionally invade my space?'

To add fuel to the fire, no apologies are offered. If someone steps on another's foot in the bus, or nearly knocks him over as he dashes for the elevator, it is unlikely that he will apologise, either in English or in Korean. This is not unique behaviour directed at foreigners. Koreans treat each other as badly, if not worse. When expatriates discuss this matter with Koreans, they are often told that they must of course know the act was unintentional, so no apology was necessary!

Physical Contact between the Sexes

According to Confucian custom, boys and girls should be separated from the age of five (which in Korea is the age of seven, since when babies are born their age is counted as one, and they become two on the first January 1 after their birth). Until very recently, schools were segregated so that few boys and girls had any friends of the opposite sex. Even today, many Koreans marry thinking that the other sex is almost another species.

Traditionally, physical contact between boy and girl was prohibited until after marriage. Overt affection was reserved for the privacy of one's own room. Today, on university campuses or in parks, couples are seen holding hands. In some areas of Seoul frequented by foreigners, one sees physical contact between the sexes. More traditional people complain that Western movies have contaminated young Koreans. But Koreans are still noticeably more conservative than their Western counterparts.

Contact between People of the Same Sex

In contrast to the strict controls put on men and women as they interact, friends of the same sex enjoy freedom of physical expression. It is common to see two women walking hand in hand. In a crowded classroom, one man may sit on another man's lap, seeming to enjoy the friendly, physical contact. Male friends may sit for some time with the arm of one on the thigh of the other.

An expatriate's first thought may be that there are many homosexuals in Korea. Koreans laugh when they hear that people from other countries may view their affectionate behaviour as a sign of homosexuality. To Koreans, it is a natural, warm way to show their feelings.

Note to Expats

A Korean generally will not touch another of the same sex unless he feels particularly friendly with that person. If someone grabs your hand or puts his hand on your leg, it is a strong indication of friendship. If it makes you very uncomfortable, there is no need to endure it; simply tell your friend that in your country such behaviour has a different meaning, and you would rather he did not touch you. Few Koreans would be offended by a sensible statement such as this.

Eye Contact

Most people are not conscious of their own culture's pattern of eye contact until they run into someone who follows a different pattern. Typical Westerners will maintain eye contact throughout a conversation, glancing away only briefly. Not to look at someone 'in the eye' is considered disrespectful or suspicious. When being scolded, it is disrespectful to look at a person of higher status.

In Korea, eye contact is kept about half the time during a conversation. When not looking at the other person, the Korean looks to either side, rather than up or down. Koreans of higher status generally keep longer eye contact than those of lower status. When one or both are angry, or during a business transaction, long eye contact is maintained. If a Korean is being scolded, he will look down slightly.

Gestures

Some gestures confuse the foreigner in Korea. The Korean 'come' is similar to the Western 'Goodbye'. When an expatriate waves good-bye from a distance, the Korean may think he is being asked to come. Koreans wave goodbye by waving their arm from side to side. The

Western version of 'come', holding palm upward, is used by Koreans only when calling a dog.

Koreans always use the right hand when handing any object to a person of higher status. To show more respect, the left hand is put, palm up, just below the elbow to support the right arm. To show the most respect, both hands hold the object as it is given or received. If a child shows a tendency to prefer his left hand, his parents and teachers will strongly encourage him to change to his right hand, as right-handed behaviour is considered most polite.

When Koreans are happy, they smile and laugh as people do the world over. But smiling holds another special meaning in Korea. It is common for a Korean to smile when he feels ashamed or uncomfortable. If your maid drops your antique crystal vase, she is likely to smile, aggravating the unenlightened Westerner further.

Traditionally, women were supposed to cover their mouths whenever they laughed or smiled. Today this is not always done, but most expatriates will still see it happen from time to time.

Silence

Koreans seem to be more comfortable with silence than Westerners. Two friends can enjoy each other's company without speaking for long periods. Strong feelings are sensed; stating deep emotions is thought to make their meaning trivial. Eating is also done in silence, as the enjoyment of a meal is believed to require one's complete attention.

Knocking on Doors

In Korea it is considered impolite to enter a room without giving some notice. Traditionally, people cleared their throats to indicate their presence. Today, they are more likely to knock on the door. If a secretary gives you permission to enter her boss's room which has a closed or even partially open door, you should not walk right in. It is considerate to knock first, twice or thrice rapidly. There is no need to wait for the person to come to the door or to respond. An expatriate can expect the same behaviour towards himself. If your door is closed and someone wants to see you, he or she will knock and then enter. Do not expect people to wait until you open the door or tell them to enter.

This custom is especially noticeable in public toilets. Sometimes the lock does not work, or there may not even be one. When a door is closed, it is polite to knock first. If someone is inside, he will knock back, or make a noise so that you know not to enter. Do the same if you do not want your toilet privacy to be invaded. Clearing one's throat loudly will communicate equally well.

– Chapter Three –

THE LIFE CIRCLE

In Korea, behaviour is determined largely by a person's age and position in society. To understand how Koreans think and behave at particular stages in their lives, it is necessary to know about how they view their responsibilities and experiences at different ages, and to have some knowledge of the ceremonies that mark them.

We shall begin with pregnancy, and then examine early childhood, school days, university life, marriage, working life, death, and finally ancestral ceremonies. Each period has particular customs, pleasures and trials.

Where relevant, advice is given to foreigners who may have the opportunity to participate in these milestones of life; for example, what sort of gifts, dress and behaviour are appropriate, and what one should say and do if invited to celebrate with the family.

It would be wise to bear in mind that every province, family and individual approaches each stage of life a little differently. The most typical stages of life are described below, but great variations occur, particularly because Korea is changing from a traditional, agricultural society to a fully developed one. Traditional customs were meaning-ful and effective when large, extended families lived near each other and when hours in the field were flexible. Some of the customs are still meaningful and practical, and the young are eager to participate in them. Others are expensive, time-consuming and cumbersome, and are being replaced by different, perhaps more appropriate practices.

PREGNANCY AND BIRTH

Koreans believe that it is their foremost duty to produce children, particularly boys, for their ancestors. Besides being a filial duty, this has also served as an insurance policy for old age, as sons were, and still are, responsible for taking care of their elderly parents physically and financially.

With the advent of a successful birth control plan, Korean couples today rarely want more than two children, and sometimes only one. But certainly the vast majority, grandparents and many young people included, prefer sons. After all, daughters result in two sorrows – once when they are born, and once when they are lost to their families through marriage.

Pregnancy

Five or ten years ago, many couples were proud to have the so-called honeymoon babies, nine months after their marriage. These days, many prefer to wait a year or two before having a child. A pregnant woman usually resides with her own family. She is treated as a somewhat helpless person who needs special care. Her nutrition, exercise, emotional health and even what she reads and thinks are all considered important for the future health of the baby. Sometimes she will work through the first months of pregnancy, but it is unusual to see a visibly pregnant woman making coffee for her boss or handing out cash at a bank.

Some old superstitions still affect the behaviour of many pregnant women, even those educated women who admit that they have no basis in fact. For example, if a pregnant woman eats chicken, it is believed that her baby may be born with 'chicken skin'. Apparently few pregnant Koreans eat chicken, because we have seen no grown ones walking around with 'chicken skin'. Another superstition claims that if a pregnant woman eats crab, her baby will bite a lot!

In cities, many women have regular prenatal health visits, just as in Western countries. In the country, this is less common. But there is no lack of advice from female relatives and neighbours. Much of it is surprisingly accurate, medically speaking. A popular seaweed soup recommended for pregnant women, for instance, contains iron and iodine, both necessary minerals for mother and child.

Naming the Baby

Names are very important to Koreans. They are believed to bring good or bad luck to the family, so fortune tellers are often consulted on this matter. The meaning of a name is very important, but since many names are in Chinese, it is sometimes difficult for other Koreans to know a name's meaning just by hearing it.

A Korean name, with few exceptions, consists of three syllables. The first is the family name. The next two are the personal name, that by which the parents call their child. Traditionally, these three syllables were Chinese words represented by Chinese characters. Recently some Koreans have adopted pure Korean names for their children.

Before a baby is born, two complete names (a girl's and a boy's) are selected, usually by the eldest male relative on the father's side. The baby's family name (surname) will be the same as his father's.

(Women retain their own family names after marriage, so a man and his wife have different family names.)

In many families, the second or third name is the same among all male cousins of the same generation. For example, Kim Chul Soo, Kim Chul Min and Kim Chul Seung could be cousins, the family name (Kim) and the generational name (Chul) being the same. The next generation of male cousins would have the same third name, for example, Kim Young Ho, Kim Jun Ho and Kim Jae Ho. The third generation would go back to using the second name as the generational name.

The Birth

When the big day arrives, most women go to hospital to deliver their babies. There is little education about childbirth, and the predominantly male doctors are not known for their sympathy, but somehow the babies are born.

The most important question is, of course, the baby's sex. Traditionally, producing a son was a wife's most important duty. If a son is born there is cause for great celebration. If a daughter is born, no one should appear too happy, lest they offend the disappointed parents-in-law or father. This preference for a son is changing, but is still very evident.

The first question asked of a new father is the sex of the baby. When that is known, he may be congratulated to the appropriate degree. If a man has a son, he is pressurised to treat his friends to an expensive meal. If the child is a girl, his friends may console him by buying him a meal.

Care of Mother and Baby

The new mother and her baby generally stay a week or less in hospital. Both in hospital, and later at home, they are looked after by an older woman. In the hospital the mother and child are separated, but at home they lie together.

Both are kept very warm, even if it is the middle of July. The mother wears long underwear so that no bare skin except her face and hands is exposed. The heating is turned on, and the reclining mother is covered with a heavy quilt. It is thought that if her skin is exposed she will get arthritis in her old age, at the very spot she bared herself. Women in their fifties love to tell stories of how they took their left arms out from under the heavy quilts in the middle of summer, and now suffer arthritis in those arms.

Diet is very important. Usually the woman's own mother takes care of her in confinement, but sometimes her mother-in-law gets the honour. The diet includes seaweed soup, about seven times a day. (Some women never regain their love for this birthday soup after their postpartum overdose.) Several types of rice gruel and other very mild, warm foods are also eaten. Korean women in the West are shocked when they are offered iced water in the hospital, or are expected to eat a normal diet.

The idea that 'bottle is best' never quite caught on in Korea, as the West had already learnt the advantages of breast milk before most Koreans had given it up. Koreans admire a mother who breastfeeds her baby. In the old days all babies were breastfed. You may occasionally run into Koreans, always the youngest in the family, who recall breastfeeding until the age of eight. While breastfeeding is the ideal, it is by no means universal. The mother is treated as a child, with little confidence shown for her mothering skills. Older women want the baby to feed continually, and are eager to supplement breast milk with formula milk. So, in fact, few young women successfully provide breast milk beyond a few months.

Strings of Pepper or Charcoal
In former times, if a boy was born, the family would hang a string of red peppers outside the door. For a girl, a string of charcoal and straw was hung. This not only announced a birth, but warned people to stay away. Not until the baby reached 21 days was it seen by outsiders.

Today, you will seldom find a string of red peppers over some-one's gate, and mothers do venture outdoors before 21 days have passed, though babies still rarely do.

The One-Hundred-Day Celebration

This celebration is a big party. The *paik il* party, as the one-hundred-day celebration is called, is held for the child who, more often than not, is rather upset about all the fuss and strangers. Rice cakes *(ddok)* are prepared, in addition to a big feast. Sometimes one party is held for the father's family, another for the mother's, and yet one more for the father's colleagues. Of course, the female family members are in-volved in the preparations. An elderly grandparent is only too happy to hold the baby during the preparations. The men enjoy the eating and drinking.

Guests always bring a nice gift to a *paik il* party. This is sometimes a set of small silver chopsticks and a soup spoon. A baby-sized gold ring and baby clothes are other common gifts. Neighbours will know about the event when they receive a plate of rice cakes and other goodies. Then they will promptly buy and bring over a gift, often clothes or a set of the Korean soft cotton underwear.

A studio photograph is also taken to commemorate this day. Traditionally, a boy was photographed naked to show off his prized 'pepper'. Girls were fully clothed. You will see many of these male one-hundred-day photographs in the windows of photography stu-dios throughout Korea.

After one hundred days, the baby is no longer seen as such a fragile human being, and may be taken outdoors. The period up to one hundred days, historically, was the most vulnerable time in a child's life, and therefore wisely treated with caution. Until that time, family and friends thought better of publicly celebrating a new life, when the child might be too weak to survive.

Note to Expats

If a Korean neighbour or friend is pregnant, congratulations are in order. The Korean greeting is '*Im shin ul chook ha hahm ni da*'. As in most other countries, if a woman merely appears to be pregnant, don't ask; it may be just a weight gain.

After the baby is born, follow the Korean custom of not visiting the home for 21 days, unless you are invited or are a close female friend of the mother's. When greeted at the door, give a bouquet of flowers and be ready to leave. You will only be asked in if the person taking care of the mother and baby decides the mother is ready for visitors.

In many Western countries, a baby gift is given as soon as the baby is born. A few Koreans do this too, and you can if you like, but it is not necessary. If you hear about the one-hundred-day celebration, you could give something around that time. For an acquaintance, clothes would be the most appropriate gift. For a close friend, or someone you have daily contact with, a set of silver chopsticks and spoon is nice.

If you have the good fortune to be invited to the one-hundred-day celebration, dress as you would to any social gathering – in conservative party clothes. Bring your gift, and be prepared to stay many hours. You will enjoy a delicious feast. The Korean greeting for 'Congratulations on your one-hundred-day celebration' is '*Paik il ul chook ha ha hahm ni da.*'

FIRST BIRTHDAY

Death before the child reached his first birthday used to be a common occurrence. Today, with excellent medical care, most children survive, but the first birthday *(ddol)* is still one to celebrate. In fact, in Korea, only one other birthday is of equal significance, the 60th birthday *(hwangap)*.

The *ddol* has some similarities with the one-hundred-day celebration, but it is on a larger scale. More food is prepared, more people are invited and perhaps even more parties given. Besides the regular feast, and the *ddok* that is served on all festivals and holidays in Korea,

*A boy and his mother sit beside the special
table prepared for his first birthday.*

another kind of rice cake is served, the *moo jee gae ddok* (rainbow),
which looks more like a layered Western cake in pink, green, brown·
and white. Being made of rice, however, it is heavier and more chewy.

First Birthday Costume

The child is dressed in the traditional Korean costume, a *hanbok (han*
means Korea, and *bok,* clothes). The brightly coloured outfit is often
made of silk. The boy's outfit consists of baggy silk trousers, shirt,
vest and jacket. He wears a black hat embossed with gold decoration.
The girl's costume is a miniature *hanbok,* such as her mother wears:
long skirt and short top with long, rounded sleeves. She, too, wears a
black hat.

These clothes are uncomfortable, so no wonder the children
usually cry when their photographs are being taken.

Photographs

These are rather prescribed. The young child, dressed in *hanbok*, sits
behind a huge table filled with food for the feast. Rice cakes and

various kinds of fruit (which are also a clear indicator of the time of year) are piled beautifully with all the other foods.

The background is usually a panelled screen, with richly embroidered birds, flowers and trees. Parents, grandparents and other siblings are included in some of the photographs – often all in *hanbok*.

The Meal

In Korea, celebrations have traditionally been held during the breakfast meal. (In the past, Korean breakfasts were no different from the food eaten at other meals.) In a farming village, this was perhaps the time when people were least tired, but in the cities, working people cannot come to a breakfast feast, so they are generally held in the evening. The women gather all day to prepare the food, and take care of the children.

Choosing the Future

Sometime during the day, the child takes part in an act believed to give a glimpse of his or her future success. Some money, a pen, a piece of thread and a book will be set before the child, and the child is allowed to grab the most attractive object. If money is picked, wealth is the child's destiny; the pen points to a future as a writer: the thread indicates long life: and the book may only be picked by a future scholar.

Sometimes parents place the child close to a particular object in an obvious bid to influence destiny!

Gifts

The traditional first birthday gift is a gold ring. This was a kind of insurance before the days of bank savings accounts. Several gold rings could always be cashed in if medical treatment was needed and the family had no money. These rings are expensive, so less wealthy family members and guests can feel comfortable pooling their money together to buy one, or instead, they can buy clothes or a toy.

Note to Expats

If your child has a first birthday in Korea, you can celebrate it whichever way you choose. Koreans will understand that your customs are important to you just as their customs are to them. But if you want a good excuse to invite some Korean friends or business associates, this would be a good time.

If you are invited to such a party, usually verbally a day in advance, or even on the day itself, drop everything and go. It is an honour to be able to celebrate this important occasion, and the food will be among the best you will eat in Korea. Dress as you would when you visit a Korean friend's home, and bring a gift: appropriate ones are a gold ring, clothes or a toy. The correct Korean greeting of congratulation on a child's first birthday is: *'Chot tol ul chook ha hahm ni da.'*

EARLY CHILDHOOD

Korean children enjoy happy, carefree lives until the age of five. This is evident from the smiles on their faces and from the way strangers treat them in public. Children are seen as valuable, entertaining, adorable and worthy of all the good things in life.

Koreans place special importance on the mother-child relationship. In expressing her love, a good Korean mother sacrifices herself completely. She stays up late if her child wants to play, even though she has to prepare breakfast at dawn for her older children. She has unbelievable patience, and tries hard to make this time a memory of joys for her child. Today, enriching her child's life with art, *Tae Kwon Do* and piano lessons are extensions of the duties of a devoted mother.

Role of the Extended Family

While the mother's role is special, all relatives have an interest in and responsibility for the children in the family. Korean children usually grow up with many caring adults in their lives, and a strong sense of security and love. Younger fathers are playing a greater direct role in their children's lives than did fathers in the past. In families where three generations live together, it is often the grandmother who looks after the child while the mother does the more difficult work of cooking, cleaning and washing. Children often spend days, weeks or even years living with a relative. This happens when both parents study abroad, or when they are busy and the child can be cared for more easily in a relative's home.

Until children start school, they rarely sleep alone, choosing instead the adult they wish to sleep with for the night. Grandmothers especially enjoy sleeping with a cuddly grandson or granddaughter.

Love and Leniency for Young Children

People who visit a home where there are children often bring gifts for them. Even strangers will buy a treat for a child. Koreans love children, no matter whose they are. Sometimes this adoration can create a problem. In restaurants, they are given free rein, sometimes so much as to disturb other patrons. Koreans do not seem to mind, but the same cannot be said of foreigners residing in Korea.

A foreigner we know went to a movie with friends and found himself next to a family with four children, the youngest aged about three. The child did not seem to want to be there, and continued crying, throwing a tantrum, and generally distracting others. Since the movie was in English with Korean subtitles, the Koreans did not mind the noise, but the foreigner was unable to hear the dialogue. He asked his Korean friend to speak to the child's parents. His friend refused (a natural Korean response). Finally, the foreigner asked the family to take the child out. They were surprised, but finally did remove the child.

Such an experience is not rare in Korea. The needs of children are often put before those of older members of the community.

Playing Outside

As most houses in Korea are built close together, and many Koreans in the city live in apartments, their children have ample opportunity to play with one another. In the days before cars, the older children

Korean children usually dress up in traditional costume on festive days, such as New Year's Day, Children's Day in May, and Chusok Day (Harvest Moon Festival) in the autumn.

would naturally watch over their younger siblings, and even if a child wandered off, everyone in the neighbourhood knew where he or she belonged.

Today, when cars share the space that children play in, and it has become impossible to know all the people in a high-rise complex, this freedom to wander as they please poses a danger to children. It is still the norm. Consequently, foreigners living in Korea will almost daily be angered by the sight of young children, some barely able to walk, playing on side streets and wandering into main streets, with no adult in sight. And, invariably, when car accidents occur, the drivers are blamed.

Note to Expats

Your own children will be a star attraction every time they go out in Korea, especially if they are light complexioned. When you take your child to the zoo, he may look at the elephants, but everyone else will be looking at him.

Koreans find children irresistible and freely touch them. Most foreign children love this attention (which comes with lots of ice cream and sweets), but some may not. If it is a problem, you may limit your time in large public places. You can shield your child from unwanted touches. You can also explain that this is the Korean way of showing their kindness and interest. Most children eventually understand this, as they will understand (probably before you do) the kind things Koreans are saying to them.

A bigger problem will be teaching your maid to treat your child with discipline. Some expatriates are lucky to find a maid who has worked with foreigners and knows the value of teaching a child what the word 'no' means. But that is rare; it is difficult for Korean maids to treat a child in a culturally different way from what they are used to. A maid will very likely buy treats if the child cries loud and long enough. And your child may quickly forget how to pick up toys or do chores.

You can help your maid by allowing her to fall back on you as an excuse: for example, 'Your mother won't let me give you ice cream before dinner.' And you can teach your child that though the maid's expectations are different, you expect your rules to be followed when you are around.

SCHOOL DAYS

In contrast to their carefree and uninhibited early childhood, once they enter school at the age of six Korean schoolchildren lead serious lives. Korean Confucian tradition considers education one of the most important things in life, both for its own sake and to better one's material and social position. During the Yi dynasty, a child from an unknown family could bring wealth and fame to his family and village by passing the government examination. This stress on education continues.

Korea has one of the highest literacy rates in the world, 96%. At present, over 95% of Korean children complete the compulsory and government-financed elementary school. Middle and high school are attended by 90% of Korean youth, though parents must pay for tuition. Just 20 years ago, students had to pass a strict examination to enter middle and high school. Today, the elementary and middle school attendance is determined primarily by a child's home address. The entrance examination to high school is not so strict, but entering a university is very competitive, so most of a child's education is aimed at getting a high score for the university entrance examination.

While children in Korean schools learn more in most subjects than their Western counterparts, much of the emphasis is on rote learning. There are between 50 and 70 students in a class, even in elementary school, making individual attention difficult. Elementary students sometimes have hours of homework every day.

Mothers are responsible for making sure that their children study.

This is especially true during high school as the university entrance examination comes closer. Mothers prepare and pack two lunches each school day, one to be eaten at lunch, the other at dinner. During that time, children usually stay at school, or at private study halls, until ten at night, and continue studying at home until after midnight.

Having Fun

The strict education system allows children little time to socialise. Their whole life revolves around studying and competing for high positions in their class. Even so, just as everywhere else in the world, Korean children do find time for fun: with their classmates on crowded bus rides home, during school athletic festivals or the bi-annual school picnics, and with their families on Sundays, their one free day in the week.

Children get a month-long vacation in the summer, and another month's vacation in the winter. The school year begins in March and ends in February.

Manners

Korean schoolchildren impress foreigners with their extreme courtesy and politeness to elders, another Confucian tradition. They bow to adults they know, and at least pretend to be happy to run errands and take care of younger children. Because of their heavy academic responsibilities and Korean mothers' self-sacrificing attitudes, one rarely sees a Korean child helping with housework.

UNIVERSITY LIFE

After three years of intense study in high school preparing for the entrance examination, university life is, for many students, a time to relax and enjoy life. Foreigners teaching at a Korean university often find the lack of academic discipline surprising, having heard how much Koreans value education. But university life is a short break between the pressures of high school and the stressful life of a worker or the self-sacrifice of motherhood.

The university one attends and the subject studied are determined primarily by the score achieved in the entrance examination, with only slight consideration given to one's interest or aptitude. Lucky and few are the ones who enter a top university to study a subject that interests them. Most students are locked into a subject they find boring, and their class preparation is kept to a minimum. These same students may spend hours in the library, studying academic subjects that they find interesting and useful, but for which they are not registered. Students often complain that homework gets in the way of their real studying.

Students spend a great deal of time on social and extracurricular activities. All universities have a variety of clubs, from broadcasting and newspaper production to drama and traditional martial arts. They demand much of a student's time, and lasting relationships are formed there.

Most male students spend a noticeable amount of time drinking and learning how to socialise with other males, a prerequisite to being an adult in Korean society. A variety of quite inexpensive alcoholic beverages are available, the rice wine *makoli* for example, so price is no barrier.

Female students generally do not drink much alcohol, but they spend hours with friends at the numerous coffee shops (see page 138).

'Meetings'

Since traditionally many students went to single-sex high schools, there was little contact between the sexes. No doubt old Confucian scholars would have approved. However, in the past ten years, the habits of the young have changed remarkably.

One new trend is a system of blind dating. Sometimes blind dates are arranged by a person who knows two young people, but more

An important part of university life is socialising to build life long connections.

often, a group of female students from one department will meet a group of male students from another belonging to a different university. The men will each donate a small article (such as a pen) to a collection, and each woman will select one of them, thereby picking the object's owner as her partner.

The conversation between 'dates' is quite predictable, ranging from hobbies and subjects being studied to family. The main factor determining satisfaction appears to be physical attraction, and after years of living relatively segregated lives, expectations tend to exceed reality. There are many stories of men, upon seeing how unattractive their partners are, leaving the coffee shop without even saving 'hello'. In Korea, such unattractive women are called 'pumpkins'.

Rarely does such a meeting turn into a real romance, or even marriage: disappointment is by far the most common result. Consequently, this practice is most usual during the first and second years.

Note to Expats

If you are a student in Korea, you can expect the pace of studying to differ from that in your home country. You might follow the Korean example and include independently directed study in your academic plans. Remember that if Koreans appear less academically inclined than many students in Western universities, at school they studied 12 hours daily for several years before reaching university level, and so they see this period of their lives as a time of relative freedom.

If you are a teacher, you will be respected, but you must also live up to your responsibility as a dedicated, humane person who is not overly critical of the host culture. As with other social interactions in Korea, you should remain very flexible, enduring sudden cancellation of classes, some 'sharing' of answers (not perceived to be 'cheating' in Korea), misunderstandings, and of course, tear gas. On the positive side, you will have a wonderful opportunity to learn about Korea at close hand and to develop close relationships with Koreans; you will also be accorded greater status and prestige than would be your due in a Western academic setting.

MARRIAGE

Single people of marriageable age in Korea are often asked '*Un chae kook soo reul muk ul soo it seul ka yo*?' ('When will I have a chance to eat noodles?') Noodles are often eaten at wedding receptions, so this is an indirect inquiry into the person's marriage plans. It can also be interpreted as pressure to marry. In Korea an individual's marriage seems to be everybody's affair.

The joining of two families and two people in marriage is about the biggest occasion in a Korean's life. The only two other events of equal importance are the first and 60th birthdays. In the past 20 years, many of the traditional marriage customs have changed and new ones have been adopted. At times, families are not sure which customs to follow.

Finding a Partner

Marriage partners may be chosen in one of two ways. Young people prefer to find their own partners, effecting 'love marriages'. Alternatively there are 'arranged marriages'.

Approximately half of the marriages in Korea today are arranged by a matchmaker, as virtually all marriages were before the arrival of Western influence. The matchmaker is usually an older female with special knowledge of the important requirements of a happy marriage. She also knows about the oriental zodiac, especially as it relates to marriage. Parents of young people go to her with all pertinent information on family background, education and social status. She then arranges a time and place for the couple and their families to meet. This is usually the coffee shop of a well-known hotel.

At first the potential bride and her parents and/or other special relatives meet the potential groom and his parents and/or special relatives. The two families talk while the young couple sit self-consciously. The woman's parents are generally concerned about the

75

man's character, his profession and how the family would treat their daughter if she married into the family. The man's parents are generally concerned about the woman's ability to get along with his family, her health (so that she can bear children and perform the responsibilities of a wife and mother) and her character. After these preliminaries they leave, and the couple may get to know each other.

In these arranged marriages, the goal is to get the best person, balancing off factors such as attractiveness, education, job, family background, and so on. If either of the young people do not want the marriage, they will not be forced into it. It should be noted, however, that there is often so much pressure from their parents, that often they marry only to escape the daily nagging.

Women are at a marriageable age from 22 to 26. If they reach 28 or 29 and are still single, they will have fewer, if any, chances to marry. Men generally marry at 25 to 28, but have some flexibility. A man over 30 will still prefer a woman under 25. Special pressure is put on young people who have a same-sex sibling ready to marry. Korean custom dictates that older sisters should marry before the younger sisters, and older brothers before their younger brothers.

If the young people like one another, or at least have no major objections, they discuss the matter with their parents. With the parents' agreement, the man will invite the woman for a few 'dates', during which they discuss issues such as whether the woman will continue working after marriage, where they will live and other future plans. These are very serious dates indeed. If all goes without a hitch, they will report their marriage plans to their parents.

Role of the Fortune Teller

At this point, customs for a love marriage and an arranged one converge. In most cases, one or both of the mothers will visit a fortune teller, who will compare the couple's birth times, days, months and years.

Should the fortune teller think their lives are not well matched, the mothers may strongly oppose the marriage. If the birth information matches, the fortune teller proceeds to advise on the best days for the marriage.

Preparing for the Marriage

Once a marriage date has been set, often only a month or two ahead, both families are very busy. As with other family matters, most of the burden falls on the females in the household. Besides choosing the wedding ceremony hall and arranging for the reception, they must prepare gifts for one another's families.

'If you have three daughters, the pillars of your house will fall down' is an old but true Korean saying. Sometimes these days, a bride's family has to sell their house to pay the dowry. Of course, the richness of the dowry depends on the groom's family. Generally, the bride has to buy Western clothes for all her groom's male relatives, including his immediate family, his uncles on both sides, his male cousins and his grandparents. She must buy Korean clothes and sometimes Western clothes as well, for all his female relatives. Then she prepares special gifts, including expensive jewellery, for her future mother-in-law, and she buys expensive quilted blankets for some of her husband's family members.

Recently, it has been the custom for some brides' families to provide the 'three keys', especially if the groom has a promising career ahead of him, such as in medicine or law. These include the keys to a new apartment or house, a new car, and a doctor's or lawyer's office. Of course, few families can afford this, but mothers of sons with respectable careers try to find such arrangements for them.

Besides gifts to the groom's family, the bride's family also provides the furnishings for their new home. As more appliances have

A bride wearing the traditional Korean costume, into which she changes after the ceremony, with dots on her face to ward off evil spirits.

become available in Korea, this is an expensive affair: a stove, refrigerator, washing machine and even a television set or sound system are included.

The groom's family also prepares gifts for the bride's family, such as clothes and jewellery, but these are usually less expensive than those from the bride's family. If the bride's family is not providing a house, as few families can afford it, and if the newlyweds will not be living with the man's parents, as many do, then the groom's family is responsible for providing a home. The costs of the wedding ceremony and reception are equally divided between the two families.

It must be noted that while this is the general custom, there are many variations, depending on the family. For example, if the groom is from a prestigious but temporarily impoverished family, his family may give few gifts. Or, if the young couple is planning to go abroad to study, the groom's parents may ask that the bride's family helps with educational expenses rather than buying furnishings.

These gifts are exchanged before the actual wedding. Although the new couple will clearly belong to the man's family, the two families try to meet and establish amicable relations.

The Hahm

Shortly before the wedding, the groom's friends carry the gifts from the groom's family to the bride's home in a wooden box, called a *hahm*. The time of delivery is prearranged with the bride's family. A friend of the groom who has had a son, or if no such friend exists, the largest friend, acts as a 'horse'. The 'horse' carries the box of gifts on his back and, true to his role, cannot speak. Another friend acts as a leader, directing the horse to go or stay.

They arrive at the bride's front gate and announce the horse is so tired that the bride's family must pay a certain amount of money for each step it takes. The women from the bride's family and the leader negotiate each step, the former having to pay money as each step is taken. It is a very noisy affair, as the groom's friends are a little drunk, and the playful bartering can go on for quite some time, to the amusement of the neighbours. Even if the bride's family lives in a modern high-rise apartment, the *hahm* can be carried up the many steps in this manner.

The men are greeted at the bride's front door by the bride's family, and inside by the bride and groom. Delicious food is prepared in advance, but the friends are usually more interested in using half the money collected to go out drinking. The other half they give to the young man as a wedding gift. A modern twist to this custom is for the bride to invite her friends to her house and, when the groom's friends go out to spend the money, they take the bride's friends with them to an expensive disco club. The bride and groom do not participate in this outing.

Hahm is not universal and many women really despise the custom, but if you live near other Korean families for long you are sure to hear the pretended arguing and know that a wedding will soon take place.

Exchange of Watches

A relatively new wedding custom is the exchange of watches. These are quite expensive and, when possible, imported. While couples often exchange rings, the rings are not always worn, so the best way to tell if a Korean man is married is to see if he has a shiny, expensive gold watch.

The Wedding Day

On the morning of the wedding, it is most common for the bride to go to a beauty parlour to be made up. Such a make-up job can transform the simplest young girl into a sophisticated model. No Korean bride looks anything but stunning. She also rarely looks like herself. Her white, Western style bridal gown is often rented from the wedding hall, and she arrives at the hall just before the ceremony begins.

Before a traditional Korean wedding, performed infrequently in recent years, a groom carries a duck, symbolising fidelity and happiness.

Brides who choose a traditional wedding do not wear white, and marry at home or in a natural setting. Such weddings are increasingly rare nowadays.

Weddings are attended by anyone who has ever known the bride or groom and is able to attend. Wedding halls are especially busy during the autumn and spring, when the guests of one wedding meet the guests of another coming in or going out. Two tables are set up to collect money, one for monetary gifts from the bride's guests, and the other for those of the groom's guests. Money is the standard wedding gift, and a close and trusted relative carefully guards the collection.

Most weddings are held at wedding halls, where a professor or distinguished friend or relative will preside, giving the couple useful advice about their marriage. Often, the guests talk during the ceremony, at least those who have managed to get into the overcrowded hall. If the wedding is held in a church, the pastor or priest presides.

During the ceremony, only the bride, groom and the person conducting the ceremony stand in front. When it ends, the newlyweds bow to each other and then to all the guests.

The bride and her family are usually sad, sometimes even tearful, during the ceremony. In a social and legal sense, the bride has left her family forever. She now has few responsibilities to her own parents, and many to her husband's family. Usually the first year of a new bride's life is very difficult. Even in the case of a love marriage, where the bride is eager to marry, she does not smile. Koreans say 'If a bride smiles before her husband on their wedding day, the first child will be a daughter', something to safeguard against. Koreans know the wedding is a very serious affair, where the couple are making the most serious promise in their lives; they should not appear happy, as if they were attending a party.

After the ceremony, photographs are taken. Then the couple quickly changes into traditional Korean wedding attire. The bride's costume includes brightly striped sleeves and a beautiful gold crown; the groom wears an embroidered blue robe. In these cumbersome clothes, the couple bows deeply to the groom's parents and other relatives. The couple drinks a toast, called *pay beck*, to their new marriage and to the groom's family.

After the ceremony, the newlyweds don traditional wedding garb, offer fruit and wine to the groom's parents, and bow deeply before them.

The Reception

Reception styles are almost as varied as the Koreans giving them. Some years ago, lavish receptions were common, but people spent far beyond their means, so the government has set limits on the amount families may spend.

When Korea had a primarily agricultural economy, weddings and wedding receptions were held at people's homes, spilling into the gardens. In cities, there is no room for such entertaining, not to mention the amount of work that would be involved, so the usual custom is to hold the weddings in wedding halls and have the receptions at nearby restaurants.

Food is served very quickly as there are so many people to serve, and often many different wedding groups eat in quick succession. It

83

is not unusual for the bride's and groom's guests to eat at different restaurants.

The main course often includes noodles, short ribs stew *(kalbi tang)*, or a traditional Korean meal with rice, soup and *kimchee* (see page 119). Rice cakes are always served, often prepared ahead of time by the women of both families.

The Honeymoon

Most weddings are held in the spring and autumn, when honeymooners can take advantage of the beautiful Korean scenery. One of the most common destinations is Cheju Island, where a taxi driver will drive the young couple to see the sights and double as a photographer. Another favourite spot is Mt. Sorak, nestled against the eastern coast. With recent relaxation of governmental restrictions on travel abroad, wealthier couples may go to Australia or Hawaii.

Honeymoons generally last for three to seven days. When the couple returns, they spend the first night in the bride's home and then move to the groom's home, where it is common for many young couples to live. This is not only for financial reasons. Since the bride has joined the new family, she needs to learn their ways: style of eating, relationships, unique family customs, and so on. This period of adjustment is usually difficult for both the bride and her mother-in-law.

Note to Expats

Since a high percentage of Koreans are of marriageable age, it is likely that Koreans you know, or their sons or daughters, will be married while you are in Korea. Invitations are sometimes sent out, but verbal invitations are more common. Koreans think that asking someone to attend a wedding directly is almost like asking for money; and asking for money is not polite. So, as with other social events in Korea, you probably will not get much advance notice. In fact, the invitation may not come directly from the couple or their family. If you hear of the wedding from others, you are more than welcome to attend. The Korean for congratulations on your marriage is '*Kyul hon ul chook ha hahm ni da.*'

Wear semi-formal clothes. Nice clothes are a sign of respect to the couple and their parents.

Koreans almost always give money instead of a gift, and it is appropriate for expatriates to do the same. The amount depends on the social status of the families and your own relationship to them. Consult with Korean colleagues or friends about the appropriate amount. The money should be offered in an envelope, with a congratulatory message written on the front, and your name on the back.

If you wish to bring your spouse, children or a special friend, feel free to do so. Since the families involved will be tied up with the wedding, and most other guests will be unable to speak your native language, you would find it more interesting if you had your own company.

WORKING LIFE

Working life probably varies more than any other of the periods of a Korean's life, for it depends on one's work and income. Here, we shall discuss only the broad categories.

Housewives

All Koreans are raised at home; all therefore have seen at first hand how busy the Korean housewife is. It seems strange, therefore, that non-housewives think working at home is the easiest job in Korea.

A housewife is at the mercy of anyone in her home. She must serve her husband's parents, whether she lives with them or not. She cooks the time-consuming recipes for the health of her family. Of course, she washes the clothes, often by hand, and keeps the house spotless, despite the layer of dust that coats her furniture each day. She caters to her husband's every whim, even when these change by the hour.

A Korean mother is responsible for meeting all her children's needs. If they are sick, lazy, poor academic achievers, or less than perfect socialisers, she is to blame. Probably her two most difficult times are when her children are preschoolers (for they are underfoot all day) and when her children are preparing for the university entrance examination. Some mothers wait up until late at night when their children are studying, serving them snacks and offering encouragement.

The housewife's need for friendship, privacy, interests and even health often have to be totally ignored for the good of her family. Unless the family is one of the lucky few who can afford to hire help, no one helps her. Men do little (but increasing amounts) of housework, and children should be able to study without the burdens of chores. If the housewife is hospitalised, a sister or other female relative comes to her home, a favour she must return in similar circumstances. If there is a word to describe the Korean housewife's life, it would be sacrifice. Her sacrifice must be done cheerfully, without complaint. While few Korean women today meet this ideal, from the Westerner's perspective they come amazingly close.

Salary Man

In Western countries, most people receive a salary, so the term 'salary man' is not used. But in Korea and Japan, this term is used often to refer to anyone who receives a salary as compared to those who run their own businesses.

Some Koreans are quite satisfied with being salary men. They enjoy the security of a stable income and the promise of continued employment for years to come. People employed by a prestigious company enjoy a certain status. Furthermore, employees have many opportunities to learn new skills, making them more employable in a different company in the future. Though salaries are often low by Western standards, workers often receive large bonuses and have access to other benefits.

Some salary men, however, feel stifled: opportunities for promotion are limited and often based more on how well one gets along with others than on ability; some complain of being overly controlled by supervisors. Such people are likely to save and learn as much as they can, then leave to start their own companies.

Salary men work long hours for their pay. A working day generally starts at 9.00 a.m. and ends at 6.00 or 7.00 p.m. Most workers put in shorter work hours one or more Saturdays per month. They do not work on Sundays. Depending on the company, a salary man gets three to seven days' vacation each year.

Independent Business People

For one reason or another, many Koreans run their own businesses. They enjoy the freedom of working for themselves, knowing that if they work hard, only they will profit.

Selling silk fabric is one way to earn a living.

87

This category includes everyone from the women who sell fruit at the outdoor markets, to the families who run small grocery stores, to the owners of international companies. They must tolerate risk, often being on the verge of losing everything. Except for people doing all the work themselves, such as fruit sellers, these independent business people spend a notable amount of time maintaining good social relationships, in order to attract and keep business. They expect the people who work for them to be at their beck and call.

Note to Expats

As an employee of a Korean, you can expect to work longer hours and spend more time socialising than you would in a Western country. As a non-Korean, you will be able to question some of your boss's practices, but if you do this too often he may hold it against you. If you head a company or office in Korea, you may have trouble getting feedback, for criticism may be misinterpreted as disrespect. Chapter Seven discusses this subject in much greater detail.

OLD AGE

One of the main doctrines of Confucianism is that respect is due to the elderly. In Korea it is clear, just by seeing them walk around, that the elderly feel pride and a kind of self-respect that is not seen in older people in Western societies. Many Koreans are shocked at how the elderly are treated in other societies.

Hwangap

Traditionally, old age began when one reached 60. According to the Chinese lunar calendar, every year in a cycle of 60 years (the sexagenary cycle) has a different name. Once every 60 years, the cycle of 60 names begins again. So, on one's 60th birthday, the calendar has travelled a full cycle back to the birth year. *Hwangap* means that one is starting the cycle over again. Modern medicine and improved living conditions have raised life expectancy to well past

60, and people continue to work beyond this age, but the 60th birthday is still the last of the three most important events in a Korean's life.

On this day, the family prepares an especially large feast, often costing thousands of US dollars. Friends and relatives gather throughout the day to congratulate the honoured person and enjoy special delicacies, including rice cakes and fresh fruit of the season, and a commemorative photograph is taken.

Modern Old Age

When families stayed close together, older people could live their days out happily, visited and honoured by their children and grandchildren. Grandmothers helped out with simple chores and grandfathers took walks with grandchildren. Even on the street, people would show respect, giving the aged a sense of importance.

Now that families are smaller and often living in different cities, things have changed. The young are not quite as willing to sacrifice

Halmoni *and* Halabuji, *walking with dignity in traditional clothes.*

their desires for the happiness of their parents. Consequently, many older Koreans feel uncared for and unimportant. Perhaps it is hardest for the current generation of elderly people, who have grown old in the expectation of being surrounded by a large family, when the reality is quite different.

This does not mean that today's elderly Koreans are not important. On the street, all elderly people are called *'Halmoni'* (grandmother) or *'Halabuji'* (grandfather), even though there are no blood ties. Seats on buses are invariably given up for an older person, and the visit of a grandparent to another city entails the preparation of special food and a big gathering of relatives. While the 60th birthday is by far the largest, in Korea all birthdays of elderly people are observed. Sons travel long distances to honour their parents on their birthdays each year. This is in contrast to very small celebrations for children's birthdays, rarely even acknowledged by relatives.

The elderly compensate for their high-pressure youth and working life by taking leisurely trips, making up a noticeable part of the group tours in Korea. At famous tourist sites throughout the country, you will see groups of 20 or 30 elderly women, wearing their pastel *hanboks,* some perhaps leaning on canes. Women at this age are free to smoke or drink, as they never could in their youth. Similar groups of old men may be seen with their horsehair hats, visiting places they had no time to see in their younger days.

Note to Expats

It would be wise to follow the Korean custom of treating the old with respect. Upon entering a Korean home, the first person to greet is the oldest.

Elder Koreans have mellowed with age, and the strict code of conduct has also been relaxed, so if they find you strange, they will stare and point you out more freely than their younger counterparts. They will also probably enjoy your company more, and accept your strange ways more readily.

Elderly Korean men, some most comfortable in traditional attire, can be seen frequently in the countryside and in the city.

If you are over 60 yourself, and quite independent, you might dislike being treated as an old person. You would probably prefer a little less respect in exchange for being considered a useful member of society. Try to accept their respect graciously and remember it was not very long ago that few Koreans actually reached the age of 60; relative to that, you are among Korean society's venerable elders.

DEATH

Korean customs surrounding death are primarily derived from the Confucian value of respect for parents and ancestors.

Koreans prefer to die at home. Every effort is made by doctors and nurses at hospitals to notify the family before a critically ill patient dies, so that he can be transported home. It is bad luck to bring the body of a deceased person home.

A deceased person is dressed in white hemp cloth and laid in a coffin. If the death occurred at home, the coffin is placed in the most honoured room, the master bedroom. If, unfortunately, the person died in hospital, the body will remain there and the wake takes place at the hospital. At either place, a screen usually hides the coffin from view. In front of the screen is a small, low table holding a photograph of the deceased and an incense burner.

The sons, particularly the eldest, stay with the body continually, hardly sleeping. They are free and encouraged to cry, especially the phrase of mourning *'I-ee-go'*. Their close friends will stay overnight, sometimes drinking and gambling to keep themselves awake.

Many come to comfort the family and pay respect to the deceased. Guests are immediately escorted to the master bedroom, where they bow to the sons and once again, more deeply, before the photograph. Incense is burned. After they leave the room, they are served with refreshments.

The body usually remains at home for three days, sometimes as long as seven, depending on the social position of the deceased. Women usually do not stay close to the body, but spend this time cooking to feed the many visitors. The deceased's favourite food is prepared for him, as if he were able to eat it.

After the wake, the body is taken to the burial site. Traditionally, the women of the house served the deceased a final meal and said goodbye at home. These days, women sometimes accompany male relatives and friends to the burial site, which is usually on a mountain and, whenever possible, facing south. Husbands and wives are buried beside each other, and many families have graveyards where sons and their wives can be buried near their parents. Unlike Western graves, the dirt covering them is shaped in a rounded mound.

Once at the burial site, the family and friends perform an ancestral ceremony. There is sometimes argument over which direction the body should be placed. The eldest son throws the first dirt over the coffin.

It is tragic if a son dies before his parents, particularly if he has no children. If there are no descendants to care for the grave, as is the case for all unmarried people, the body is cremated and the ashes often spread over a river or on a mountain.

Another exception to customary burial is the Buddhist funeral, where the body is cremated.

Note to Expats

When someone you know or the relative of someone you know dies, it is appropriate to visit the deceased. No gift is necessary, but you may give a little money (between 20,000 and 50,000 won) in an envelope. Donations are made at a table inside the home or hospital room. You can express condolences, burn incense and, if you wish, bow to the photograph of the deceased.

Few expatriates attend funerals, but if you are especially close to the deceased or the family, there is no harm in going. The ceremony is held at home and a rented bus will carry the body, family and friends to the burial site.

ANCESTRAL CEREMONIES

The custom of ceremonies to honour deceased relatives came to Korea from China even before Confucianism. It was reinforced when Confucianism became a major force influencing social behaviour. The ceremonies stressed filial piety and helped strengthen the bonds between living family members.

As with other customs in Korea, ancestral ceremonies vary widely, depending on the particular family customs, religion, and on the home of the first known family ancestor, who may have lived thousands of years ago. The ceremonies are so complex that many Koreans cannot say for sure what their particular family customs require on these important cerenonies.

Ceremonies at the Grave

Ceremonies are performed in front of the grave when the body is buried. They are then regularly performed in the spring (Hanshik Day), autumn (Chusok), and sometimes at whichever New Year the family celebrates. The oldest living male descendant is the leader responsible for the ceremony.

On the designated day, the male descendants (and sometimes their wives) go to the graves of their parents and grandparents, which are usually located next to each other. A small, low table or special cloth is placed in front of the graves and special food is set on it. Red food is placed towards the east, white towards the west.

Traditionally the leader bows twice before the table. These ancestral bows require that one lowers one's head to the ground. He then pours a glass of rice wine over the grave and bows twice with the other male descendants. Finally, the women, if any are present, bow two or four times. Bowing an odd number of times is unlucky. Sometimes families today vary the protocol, with men and women bowing at the same time.

After the initial bowing, the graves and surrounding areas are cleaned up. Grass is cut and flowering plants are sometimes planted.

The line-up for the traditional bow before the ancestral graves. Notice that in this most respectful form, the heads almost touch the ground.

Twenty or thirty minutes later, the bowing ceremony is repeated. The offering of food and alcohol is then consumed.

Though the ceremony is serious, it is not sad. It is a time for the descendants to remember their ancestors, to pay respect, and to feel the importance and bonding of the current family. Children sometimes attend, and though they are required to be quiet, it is an enjoyable occasion for them, not unlike a picnic.

Ceremonies in the Home

Ancestral ceremonies are held at the home of the oldest surviving male, three or four times a year: on the death anniversary, on New Year's Day, Chusok and, for the first three years after the death, on the deceased's birthday. The home ceremony is similar to the graveyard one, except that bowing is before a photograph of the ancestor instead of the grave.

Notable Exceptions

When Christian missionaries came to Korea, they forbade ancestral ceremonies as a form of idolatry. Today most Christians do hold some kind of ceremony but it is far simpler than the traditional ceremony. Churches are divided on the issue.

When Korea had primarily an agricultural economy, sons lived near each other and near to the family graves. It was easy for them to perform the ceremonies many times each year. This is of course no longer possible.

Chapter Four

ANNUAL PASSAGE – SEASONS AND FESTIVALS

Korea's beautiful countryside makes the four clear seasons particularly striking. Each season lasts about three months. The scenery appears to be changing continually, and if the winter seems too cold or the summer too long, one can take heart in the fact that the next season is just round the corner.

Spring

This especially welcome season comes earlier in the south, gradually spreading to the north. The first sign is the bright yellow forsythia flowers which line streets, surround houses and decorate expressways. Then, one by one, other spring flowers make their appearances, resulting in four to six weeks of blooms. The weather is cool at first, and sometimes wet, but gradually becomes warmer.

Small strawberries in the markets are another sign of spring. As the season progresses, they give way to large, lush ones and later to boysenberries. By the time the yellow melon appears, one can tell summer is on the way.

Spring is a beautiful time to travel in Korea; the Chinhae Cherry Blossom is an unforgettable sight, as is a visit to any temple.

Summer

The clear spring days are often followed by a two-week spell of rainy weather, beginning at about the end of June. Sometimes the heavy summer rains result in floods.

After the rainy season, the really hot and humid weather begins. This is when straw mats for ventilated seating and the beautiful Korean fans come in handy. Highs in Seoul often reach 26° Centigrade (80° Fahrenheit). Cold watermelon and sweet juicy peaches are some consolation in the intense, overbearing heat, which however lasts only a few weeks, and sometimes not even that long. By the beginning of September, the evenings turn refreshingly cool.

Autumn

The height of autumn, much acclaimed by visitors to Korea, lasts a good month. As in spring, there is a progression of colours, making even the humblest home a castle. This season is also an especially good time to explore Korea. The temples, always located on a picturesque mountain, couldn't be more beautiful. Nae Jang San in North Cholla Province is an especially popular place, as is Sorak Mountain on the northeastern coast.

Autumn is marked by crisp, sweet apples in the market, along with the unique Korean pear (in many places it is known as the Asian pear), huge purple grapes and the fragrance of roasting chestnuts on the street.

Kimchee *pots store* kimchee *through the winter. When temperatures drop to freezing, the pots are buried.*

For housewives, one of the most important autumn events is Kimjang. This is the time for making the all-important dish of *kimchee* that is to last all winter. Markets are full of heaps of Chinese or *napa* cabbages, radishes, green onions, red peppers and garlic, the main ingredients for *kimchee*. These foods are pickled and stored in the ground in large clay pots. In the warmer southern provinces, more salt is used to preserve the *kimchee,* accounting for the distinct flavour variations in different parts of the country. These days, supermarkets are well stocked with fresh vegetables all year round, so housewives do not make as much *kimchee* as they used to in the autumn. For many

Koreans, however, Kimjang *kimchee* is the most delicious *kimchee* of the year.

Winter

Winter is milder in the far southern regions than further north, the snow not even reaching Pusan. Other regions receive varying amounts of snow. Watching Koreans dispose of snow can baffle the recent arrival. They sweep the snow from the curb into the street. Then as the cars run over it, the snow melts and disappears. Most Western countries sweep the snow off the streets.

As energy is expensive, many public buildings and homes in Korea are heated insufficiently for the pampered expatriate. To compensate, Koreans sell lightweight cotton underwear that adds another five degrees Centigrade to your body temperature.

The heating system in Korean homes is unique. A series of pipes lies beneath the floor and hot water (in the older homes, hot air) runs through the pipes, making the floor pleasantly warm. This is called an *ondol* floor. The warmth rises naturally. The Korean tradition of sleeping, eating and sitting on the floor makes this a peculiarly sensible heating system. Most apartments and homes where expatriates live are also heated this way.

As elsewhere, the fruits of winter are sparse. Mandarin oranges from Cheju Island are abundant, and some hardy apples are still available. In late November a unique citrus fruit, *yooja*, can be bought, layered with honey or sugar and set aside. Then, in the cold winter, it is an especially welcome tea, *yooja cha*.

HOLIDAYS AND FESTIVALS

Koreans really know how to celebrate. No expense or energy is considered too great when guests are visiting to celebrate a happy occasion. The tendency is to spend too much, in proportion to income, so as not to offend guests or appear less successful than one would wish.

Women have all the responsibilities associated with holidays. In fact, many men do not even know how holidays are celebrated. They merely attend, eat, drink and drink more. Female family members, particularly the daughters-in-law, arrive the night before to help the hostess, sleeping overnight.

Following the Confucian system, holidays are celebrated in the oldest family member's home. This is usually the oldest son's home, where the grandparents also live. The sons all gather together while their wives cook. That family's daughters, if married, would be working in their husbands' family homes. Occasionally, a couple will try to get to the wife's parents' home after they have celebrated for an appropriate period at the husband's family home. Of course, by this time, the wife is exhausted and unable to enjoy herself much. But then holidays, like everything else, are not designed to provide enjoyment for women.

New Year's Day   *2-day National holiday 1 and 2 January*
By far the biggest holiday in Korea, this is like combining everyone's birthday (this is the day everyone adds a number to their age), Christmas and New Year into one day. Traditionally this was celebrated on the lunar New Year, but the government, in an effort to celebrate like many other countries, forced people to work on that day, and so many families changed their celebration to coincide with the solar calendar. But more families continued to resist the change until 1985, when the government eventually acknowledged their unsuccessful attempts to change the celebration and made lunar New Year a national holiday (Folklore Day) as well. The first month of the lunar year is also, confusingly, called January.

Currently families celebrate the traditional holiday on one of the two days, but the customs are the same. The most important feature is bowing deeply to one's ancestors and elders. Food is set before photographs of the family ancestors, and the family members bow deeply, first to them, next to the grandparents, and then to the parents.

101

Younger sons and their wives bow to older brothers and their wives. The children in one nuclear family bow together. This special bowing, called *sae bae*, is often done in traditional clothes, especially by women. Recently, it has become more common to see men in *hanboks* on family holidays, too.

When children bow deeply to their elders, they are usually given money, called *sae bae tone* (*tone* means money). College-age cousins use this to go to the discos later in the day.

After the *sae bae*, breakfast is served. The food includes dumpling soup (*ddok guk*), rice cakes, fruit, a rice punch (*shikae*) and a punch made of dried persimmon and honey (*soo jung gwa*). Two kinds of rice wine are traditional for this day: *makoli* and *dong dong ju*.

Perhaps more than other holidays, when men often segregate themselves from women and children, this is a day for family activities. One of the most popular games played by Koreans of all ages is *yoot*. Four wooden sticks, one side flat and one side rounded, are thrown up into the air. Players take turns throwing them up and are awarded points, depending on how the wooden sticks land.

Another popular activity in the country, especially for the boys, is kite flying. The brightly coloured kites are strikingly beautiful against the clean white snow. For girls there is the traditional Korean see-saw. (These and other traditional Korean folk games are described on pages 127–130.)

On solar New Year's Day, if there is time, or in the days that follow, Koreans visit the homes of those they respect. Students will visit teachers, workers their boss or anyone older who has been (or whom they hope will be) of particular help. These people are honoured by a deep bow. Visits are expected, so each family keeps plenty of refreshments on hand.

Note to Expats

Take a walk in the streets if you are in Korea during the solar and lunar New Years. You will see hundreds of traditional *hanboks* and the

Sae bae. *Grandson and granddaughter bow deeply before their grandparents in the traditional New Year's greeting.*

excitement in the air is infectious. Be warned however that all stores will be boarded up. Stock up on groceries and other essentials.

When invited to a Korean's home, you too can dress in a *hanbok* if you feel comfortable doing so. You may enjoy the family emphasis, which is unlike many Western New Year customs, where meeting friends and drinking are the focus.

If you wish to usher in the New Year with a few drinks, several first-class hotels offer enjoyable parties.

Folklore Day   *National holiday*
This is the traditional date to celebrate the lunar New Year, made a legal national holiday in 1985.

Poh Reum Nal   *January/February (lunar)*
As more Korean housewives concern themselves with non-domestic
activities, many families do not celebrate this day. It comes on the first
full moon of the lunar new year.
    Traditionalists go vegetarian, eating only grains and vegetables.
Ogok bap is eaten for good luck in the year ahead. It consists of five
ingredients: rice, sticky rice, kidney beans, soy beans and millet. The
housewife prays to the moon for a good year. Then she wraps this
special rice in seaweed and leaves, hanging some of it at the gate.
Children eat the seaweed-wrapped rice from their neighbours' gates
and enjoy the beauty of the full moon.
    Boys play a game at this time. They light a fire in a can, tie a string
to it and swing it around to make a circle of light.

Independence Day   *National holiday, 1 March*
This holiday observes the 1 March 1919 Independence Movement
against Japanese colonial rule. There is an annual reading of the
Korean Proclamation of Independence.

Arbour Day   *National holiday, 5 April*
There is an old belief in Korea that anything planted on this day will
flourish. After the Korean War, it became especially important, as
hundreds of mountains had been completely burned in the hunt for
communists. On Arbour Day, you will see groups of government
officers, company workers and schoolchildren planting trees. Koreans will often plant trees and flowers in their gardens, and apartment
dwellers buy flower boxes to bring some nature into the towering
cement structures they call home.

Hanshik Day   *5 or 6 April*
Hanshik literally means 'cold food'. According to legend, long ago in
China lived a man, Kai Ja Chu, who was very loyal to his king. Jealous
of his devotion, the other subjects forced him from the king's

presence. If Kai Ja Chu could not be with the king, he wanted to live in solitude, so he hid in the mountains. The king searched for him, without success. Upon hearing Kai Ja Chu was hiding in a mountain cave, the king set fire to the mountain to drive him out. Kai Ja Chu died in the fire. In admiration of his loyalty, the remorseful king and people decided to honour him by eating only cold food on the anniversary of the fire, a Chinese custom that eventually came down to Korea.

Today in Korea, this day is often set aside to tend ancestors' graves. The women pack a picnic lunch (not always cold) and the family heads for the burial site, usually on a scenic mountain slope and reached on foot.

At the grave, the ancestral ceremonies are performed and the graves are weeded and reshaped after the winter. While the ceremony is serious, the family thoroughly enjoys the picnic and the beginnings of spring weather. If a family is unable to go to the grave on Hanshik Day, members will designate another day to go.

Note to Expats

If you plan to travel out of the city on this day, you can expect the roads to be crowded with traffic, especially as it is not a national holiday but business as usual. Korean families hiking through the mountains make a pleasant sight.

Children's Day   *National holiday, 5 May*

It is only to be expected. A country where children are loved so well would surely set aside a special day for them. On this day, children do anything they please: go to amusement parks, visit the zoo, have a picnic, or participate in one of the many special programmes organised just for them.

Korean children also receive gifts from their parents on this day. If you have children, they would doubtless be happy if you followed this custom. As on other holidays, be warned that traffic in and out of the cities will be heavy and places catering for children very crowded.

Parents' Day   *8 May*
This day was traditionally set aside to honour mothers, indicating perhaps the strong affection Koreans have for their mothers. Somewhere along the way, it became Parents' Day so as not to neglect the fathers. Children often buy a corsage for their mother and some small gift for their father.

Teachers' Day   *15 May*
Teachers who have a special place in this Confucian-oriented society are honoured on this day. Students give them small gifts or a corsage, and university students sometimes treat their professors to lunch.

Buddha's Birthday *National holiday, 8th day of the 4th lunar month*
On this day, Buddhists visit temples to pray. Families buy a colourful lantern, attach a ribbon with the family's names, and hang it at the Buddhist temple. In the evening a lantern parade is held.

Memorial Day   *National holiday, 6 June*
A day in remembrance of Koreans who died in service to their nation. Memorial services are held at the National Cemetery in Seoul.

Constitution Day   *National holiday, 17 July*
This day commemorates the adoption of the Constitution for the Republic of Korea in 1948.

Liberation Day   *National holiday, 15 August*
Besides commemorating the beginning of the Republic of Korea in 1948, this day celebrates the freedom from the Japanese on this same day in 1945.

Chusok   *National holiday, August (lunar) 3 days*
Harvest Moon Festival and Korean Thanksgiving are two other names for this holiday, the second most important one in Korea.

Three generations prepare song pyon, *rice cakes shaped like a moon, for the* *Chusok festival.*

Families visit ancestors' graves, set out food and bow. Among special foods from the fall harvest are rice cakes *(song pyon)*, shaped like a half moon.

A dance performed at this time, especially popular in South Cholla Province, is the *kanggang suwolae*. It originated when the Japanese were invading the southern coast during the 16th century and Korean women joined hands in a circle and danced around, to give the impression to distant Japanese soldiers that there were many Korean soldiers.

The Chusok moon is supposed to be the most beautiful of the year, so many people stroll outdoors to enjoy the bright full moon.

Armed Forces Day   *1 October*
Military parades are often held in Seoul on this day.

107

National Foundation Day *National holiday, 3 October*
Called Kae Chun Chul in Korean, this day's literal translation is Sky Opening Day. This commemorates the day in 2333 BC when legendary Tan-gun founded the Korean race.

Hangul Day *9 October*
This day celebrates the creation in 1446 of *hangul,* the phonetic Korean alphabet that gave the race its literacy. Until that time, there were only the difficult Chinese characters no one but the elite scholars could read.

Christmas Day *National holiday, 25 December*
Christmas is very visible throughout Korea, with Christmas lights and decorations in the market, decorated trees in many coffee shops and hotels, and bargain sales at the major department stores. For the Christians in Korea (about 25% of the population), as for Christians everywhere, this is a religious holiday. For the others, it is another excuse to get together with friends for drinks.

Note to Expats

For the expatriate who is unable to go home for Christmas, this holiday can be a lonely time. Separated from loved ones, no quantity of tinsel, greeting cards or Santa Clauses can create that familiar spirit. Certainly, the parties and programmes organised by Korean and foreign organisations do not appear to fill this gap.

Many expatriates have found it more helpful to start new traditions than cling to the old ones. Santa Claus can never get into a 13th floor apartment with a guard and no chimney. Getting together with other Westerners, making some non-traditional but special food and observing those customs that are transferable to Korea are excellent ways to build memories in a foreign land. Several churches offer special services in English, and even at the Korean churches you will be able to hear the familiar Christmas melodies.

Chapter Five

ENJOYING LIFE

Koreans are eager for expatriates to join them in their good times, and opportunities abound for fun in Korea. It may be because the country is so crowded and many of the social rules very strict, or perhaps it is because Koreans have one of the longest working weeks in the world. Whatever the reason, Korean men, in particular, consider fun a necessity if they want to keep their sanity. They do not seem to require much: a few friends, some alcohol, tasty food or an interesting place to see, all provide the relaxation they need.

In this chapter Korea's unique drinking customs, the perceptions of friends, food and the customs surrounding it, a summary of the vacations Koreans take, and details of several traditional Korean folk games are all discussed. Each part includes advice on etiquette and a few useful Korean words and phrases when necessary.

DRINKING

While the role of alcohol has diminished somewhat in recent years, for many Korean men drinking remains an integral part of most kinds of fun. Whether attending a one-hundred-day celebration, camping, socialising or trying to establish an amicable business relationship, liquor is almost indispensable, at least when socialising with men over the age of 40.

Korea has one of the highest per capita rates of alcohol consumption in the world. This is especially notable since almost all the drinking is done by half the Koreans – the male half. Drinking is difficult to avoid in Korea and learning the drinking customs is not easy.

Purpose

Any reason is a good reason for saying *'Han chan hapshida!'* (Korean for 'Let's have a drink.') If it's raining, it's a good time to drink, but a sunny day is an equally good excuse. When bad luck descends on a person or his friends, the best way to forget is to drink. If one just got paid, it's necessary to drink, but if one has no money, it's appropriate to drink. Good times, bad times, average times – all are perfect for drinking.

Many Korean men believe that the best way to get to know a person is to drink with him. They believe that adults show the world a kind of mask, appearing to be as others expect them to be. To know a person's true self, they must see him 'under the influence'.

Drinking is often a necessary prelude to any business. It may be difficult to trust a business partner until a few drinks have been shared. Sometimes the only way to resolve a sensitive problem or close a touchy business deal is over a generous amount of wine. People who do not drink as much as their counterparts are sometimes thought to be hiding something, afraid to let down their defences. Many Koreans would prefer not to drink so much, but not to drink, or to stop drinking too soon might ruin the mood for everyone.

This emphasis on drinking for social and business reasons goes back to the Unified Shilla period, if not before. There are even Confucian ceremonies demonstrating the proper way to become drunk. Fortunately, there is a trend among younger Koreans away from such heavy drinking. In the younger crowds, abstinence or moderate drinking are more acceptable than for people in the older generation. Still, drinking continues to pervade many aspects of the lives of most Korean males.

Drinking Customs

The expatriate may be baffled the first time he goes drinking with a Korean. There are several well-kept rules.

- The person of lower status, or the host of the event, will offer a glass to the most honoured person.
- If the status or age difference is very great, he will offer the glass with two hands, or support the right hand with the left.
- The person receiving the glass, depending on his status, will also receive it with two hands or with the right supported by the left.
- The giver then pours the alcohol into the glass held by the receiver.
- As the drinking continues, everyone is offered a glass, which is then filled.
- After one finishes one's own glass, it is customary to give the same glass to another person. During the course of an evening, people are careful to exchange glasses with everyone else.
- One should not add alcohol to a glass that is partially filled, or fill one's own glass.

Luckily, with all this drinking, food is also consumed. These appetisers, collectively called *anjoo*, may include dried beef, dried fish, nuts or even fruit. Some places offer an *anjoo* menu. At other places, *anjoo* is brought to your table even if not ordered, but even so it is not free of charge.

The Role of Women in Social Drinking

Traditionally, a good Korean woman didn't drink. This custom is changing, especially among college women who often enjoy drinking alongside their male classmates. Younger married women can be found drinking moderately with their friends or husbands, but heavy-duty drinking is mostly left to the men.

A different sort of woman may be found in some drinking establishments. These young, beautiful women are hired to sit with an equal number of men, pour their drinks and make friendly conversation. The price of their company runs from about US $15 to $60 per woman. Do not confuse them with prostitutes. It goes without saying that wives and girlfriends are not welcome at such places.

Gisaengs

Gisaengs, dressed in traditional Korean clothes and found only in *gisaeng* houses, have a long and important history in Korea. They used to be the only educated women. Not only could they write poetry and practise Chinese calligraphy, they sang and danced. Trained in special schools, their job was to entertain aristocrats at parties.

While these women were always from the lowest social class, there are several instances of *gisaengs* who became heroines. One story goes how, after the Japanese invaded the southern coast of Korea in the late 15th century, the famous *gisaeng*, Non-Gae, entertained a Japanese general. She convinced him to take a walk along a cliff by a river. At an opportune moment, she clasped her arms around the general and fell into the river with him. They both died. You can visit the spot in Jinju.

While the number of *gisaengs* has substantially diminished, elegant *gisaeng* houses still exist in Korea. Gracious women pour drinks, put morsels into their customers' mouths, dance, and sing.

These houses are extremely expensive, bills sometimes running to many thousand US dollars for a small group of people. Companies entertain potential clients in the splendour of *gisaeng* houses and wealthy foreigners can sample a side of Korean culture there.

Singing

When Koreans drink, it is rarely just one beer after a hard day's work. Oblivious of work the morning after, drinking often continues until late into the night. As the evening progresses, the most honoured person will be asked to sing solo.

To the expatriate, this can be quite an unnerving experience. It does not matter if you cannot sing: make sure you know the words to one short song. There have been cases when an innocent foreigner has managed to avoid singing, but remember this is done at some social cost. It is far better to sing a few lines of 'Mary Had A Little Lamb' and be done with it.

Sometimes, listening to other singers can be worse than singing yourself. The majority of Koreans sing exceptionally well, and their presentation can be quite interesting, but when all you want is to go home, and every one of your 15 companions is waiting to perform, you will not find it so entertaining.

Singing while drinking is an old custom, but a new twist to this practice is the karaoke bar. This is a bar that provides a stage and taped music or a live band to accompany anyone willing to pay a small fee. For a few moments, the most ordinary person can pretend to be a famous singer with all the customers at the bar providing his real audience. At other drinking places, groups of friends rent private rooms (and often an equal number of hired women), and small bands rove from room to room, accompanying the customers.

Refusing a Drink

Considering the amount of alcohol imbibed, there may be times when one is tempted to refuse. This borders on anti-social behaviour.

Koreans have the same problem, as there is often one person urging everyone else to drink one more glass, but being Koreans, they go ahead and drink, even if it means becoming sick.

An expatriate has the advantage of being able to 'play dumb' about all these drinking customs. It might even be understood that your own custom requires you to go home to your wife. Some foreigners and Koreans have poured unwanted alcohol surreptitiously into a local plant. In less refined establishments, alcohol could be spilt, quite accidentally of course. Holding a full glass and drinking slowly also makes it less likely that another will be poured for you. If all else fails, you can say you are taking traditional Korean medicine *(hanyak)* and so cannot drink. You may also say your religion discourages drinking. This is a common acceptable excuse among Korean men.

Drinking Behaviour

While some degree of control should be kept, no matter how much is consumed, one sometimes sees a person who, by Western standards, has lost control. Physical fights, loud arguing and men supporting their far-gone drinking buddy are features of popular drinking areas.

In apartment blocks, understanding neighbours are expected to tolerate loud laughter, singing and fights. It is unthinkable to call the police to curb the disturbance. Much drunken bad behaviour is excused.

FRIENDSHIP

In the Korean way of thinking, a real friend is as intimate as a family member. A friend cannot be made easily and, once made, must never be neglected. Koreans often view Western friendships as fickle and shallow.

A friend is someone to relax with (relaxing is not easy in a family setting), to listen to your problems, to truly understand you, and on whose generous help you can count at any time in your life – and vice versa. The most reliable friends are made early in life – during elementary, middle or high school. Some Koreans believe that after that time one's heart cannot fully open to another human being. Some friends are made at university, but rarely any time after that.

Such friends will keep in touch through years of separation. The obligations are almost as great as those of a family member. People may give thousands of dollars to their less fortunate friends. A Korean who does not live up to his responsibility as an intimate friend would lose face among other friends. These close friendships, similar for men and women, and always between people of the same sex and age, happen less than ten times in most Koreans' lives.

Alumni

Another special though different relationship exists between Koreans who graduate from the same school. This could be the same kindergarten, school or university. Regardless of whether they knew each other during school, they can use the intimate language form of old friends. Those who graduated before a Korean student *(sonbae)* may be in good positions to help him get a job. They would be very comfortable working with him and he, in turn, would be obligated to show respect, and to support them in whatever they thought or did. Even at university, a second year student can call a first year student by name, but the first year student must call the second year student *'hyung'* or *'noona'* (older brother or older sister). Someone who attends your school after you is called *hoobae*.

So strong is the tie between Koreans from the same school or university, that they will try very hard to go to a well-known university, one with powerful, influential alumni. If a Korean were given a choice between hiring a person from his university or a better qualified person from another, he would frequently choose the former. Consequently, many companies hire several employees from the same university, perhaps the same one attended by the company president. It makes relationships a little smoother.

115

There are drawbacks to this system. Not only does it perpetuate like-minded thinking, it also makes innovation unlikely because the new employees are unable to question any bad practices perpetrated by their seniors.

To maintain the strong relationship between alumni, meetings are held regularly. Alumni of the same department and year may meet monthly. At the end of the year there are often parties for all of the alumni of one university. There are even alumni associations for Koreans who attended a particular university from another country, such as Germany or America.

Social Relationships between Adults

Once adulthood is reached, Koreans certainly do not avoid social interaction. In fact, much of an adult Korean's time is spent socialising and maintaining good relations with people other than his close friends. But the nature of these friendships is very different from that between close, long-term friends.

There is more of a give-and-take aspect to such relationships. A person drinks with someone whose father might be able to give his son a job. Relationships with neighbours are cultivated so that they can protect one another's homes. Colleagues at work meet to keep relationships in the office smooth. And of course businessmen 'work' late into the evening drinking with potential clients.

These relationships can be fun, and Koreans truly admire or respect each other. The obligations of this type of friendship are however entirely different from those of childhood friendships; there is an understanding that they can be ended more easily if one person is offended or if neither person sees any need for continuing the relationship.

Note to Expats

Relationships between Koreans and expatriates can fall into friendship patterns from either culture, or, more often, a combination of the two. Some Koreans will view the expatriate as someone to benefit from: a partner for conversation practice; a free temporary home if he visits the foreigner's homeland; a means of obtaining a visa to that country. Some expatriates have felt used, not realising that many relationships between Koreans are also established primarily for utilitarian reasons.

There are also Koreans who welcome the relative openness of adults from other countries, and they respond by opening themselves, usually more intimately than they would to their fellow Koreans. Expatriates with such relationships feel especially fortunate, for the deep kindness shown in such a friendship is more than they are likely to experience in their own country.

No matter what kind of friendship exists between a Korean and yourself, it will enrich your stay in Korea; having only expatriate friends, one is isolated from real Korean thinking. Sometimes the most natural friendships between the two cultures arise between expatriates and Koreans who have lived in the expatriates' country, and who are thus sympathetic to the difficulties of living outside one's culture. Koreans who have lived abroad also often understand expatriates' frustrations with some aspects of Korean life.

FOOD

Koreans eat flavoursome, spicy side dishes, served attractively with their staple, rice. Many people assume that Korean food is similar to Chinese or Japanese food. The only thing all three countries have in common is their staple. Koreans depend heavily upon the spices they use when cooking everything from cucumber to fish and beef. These include red pepper, garlic, green onion, soy sauce and sesame oil.

Korean food may appear strange to expatriates at first, but it is rare to find one who does not eventually succumb and enjoy it immensely. Perhaps that is why Korean restaurants are popping up all over the world. The variety of colours, textures, tastes and smells are sure to have something that pleases every palate.

The Meaning of Food

Most Koreans over the age of 60 have experienced times when the next meal was not guaranteed. During the Korean War, sometimes the only thing to eat was barley and *kimchee*, the spicy pickled cabbage essential to the Korean diet; little wonder that food takes on a special significance in Korea.

There seems to be a preoccupation with food that goes beyond mere enjoyment and becomes directly connected to health. Mothers and grandmothers spend a great deal of time making sure that family members get the nutrition they need. When something considered especially healthful, like beef, is served, they will pass it up so that their husbands and sons can eat more of it. It is sometimes difficult to encourage a grandmother to eat much. She hates to waste any nutrition on herself when there are young children who need it more.

One of the most appreciated gifts is some kind of nutritious food, for example honey or ginseng, both of which are expensive in Korea. The line between medicine, especially the traditional herbal medicine called *hanyak,* and food is very fine. People with particular ailments are instructed to eat particular foods, as though they were medicine.

In contrast to Western countries where a family can usually buy enough of any food to satisfy all family members, Koreans value each item of food as though it were rationed. Even at restaurants, hosts will often put meat on their guests' plates to show that they are concerned with their health. Children grow up hearing *'Moko, moko',* meaning 'Eat, eat'. Most expatriates would be astonished if when they were aged 40, their 65-year-old mothers were still saying 'Eat! Eat!' at every meal, but Koreans do not mind, since love is behind the insistence.

As a guest in Korea, you are likely to be encouraged to eat more than you want. Koreans have no wish for all expatriates to get fat (though there is real danger of this, given the delicious Korean food); they are just showing their concern that you stay healthy. Fortunately, it is also polite not to eat everything that is offered.

Typical Korean Food

Koreans make no distinction between breakfast, lunch and dinner food. The main item is rice, of the partially sticky variety that the Japanese eat. This is eaten with various side dishes.

Kimchee is served with every meal, and many Koreans claim they get withdrawal symptoms if a day passes without it. This has caused some problems for Korean students studying abroad as the smell of *kimchee* permeates a dormitory refrigerator.

Kimchee can be made of almost any vegetable, but usually it is made of Chinese or *napa* cabbage which is rinsed with salt water and left to ferment overnight. Then spices and herbs are added, including garlic, red pepper, green onion and ginger. It has an indescribable, distinctive taste, and most people cannot understand what is so special about it at first. But it grows on you.

There is a story of an American prisoner of war who spent five years in a North Korean prison. When he was released, he told his wife 'You have got to learn how to make *kimchee.*' Koreans are very glad to hear that foreigners like their national food.

Besides rice and *kimchee*, every meal includes soup, the only liquid taken with the meal. The soup, which is normally served hot,

may contain a number of items, such as fish, bean paste, beef, and mung beansprouts.

All the other foods at the meal are called *pan chan* or side dishes. Modern housewives aim to have five or more side dishes at each meal. Usually this includes a variety of vegetables, lightly cooked with the Korean spices, and may or may not include fish, pork or beef. Beef is expensive in Korea, even for expatriates, so many Korean families only serve it on special occasions.

Noodles are also eaten, at times in place of rice. There is a wide variety of rice and flour noodles, sometimes made at home. Ready-to-cook noodles may be bought in the market.

Table Manners

Traditionally, the men of the house were served first. They ate on low, lacquered tables that were set in the kitchen and carried into another room for the meal. (Koreans used the same room for eating, visiting and sleeping.) Korean women traditionally sat by the men, watching them as they ate, ready to get them anything else they needed. Only when the men were finished would the women and children eat.

These days, men, women and children usually eat together. Families may use either the Western style table and chairs or the traditional low table. Hot rice is served in individual bowls, placed to the left of the diner, and soup is served in another bowl, always to the right of the rice. The various side dishes are set on small plates. If there are very many people, two or more plates of the same food are set out, to make passing unnecessary. Stainless steel or silver chopsticks are used, with a large soup spoon.

The most honoured person (usually the oldest) takes the first bite. During meals, it is considered impolite to talk much; the food should be enjoyed without distraction. This silence may seem strange to expatriates. In fact, the meal is not silent. To show your appreciation of the food, slurping of soup and noodles is totally acceptable. Some older Koreans burp at the end of the meal, as a sign of satisfaction.

Many Koreans today enjoy eating their meals in the traditional way, sitting on cushions at low tables.

Seasonal fruit is served at the end of the meal, cut into small pieces. It is eaten with a fork or toothpicks. (Eating any food with fingers is considered impolite.) Sweets and desserts are generally eaten as snacks, not during main meals.

Foods to Try

- **Bee Bim Bap** A huge bowl is filled with rice, and small piles of various colourful vegetables are layered on top. A barely cooked egg sits to one side. Koreans add a generous amount of hot pepper paste to their individual bowls and mix it all together.
- **Bulgogi** Thin strips of beef that have been marinated in soy sauce, garlic, green onions and sugar, then barbecued, often right at your

table. This food is served on special occasions. Since Koreans have correctly heard that foreigners like this food and because they wish to offer guests the best, expatriates tend to be served *bulgogi* often.

- **Chop Chae** A mixture of clear noodles and a variety of cut-up vegetables and meat. A dish expatriates invariably fall in love with.
- **Kalbi** Barbecued beef ribs, prepared in a similar way to *bulgogi.*
- **Kalbi Chim** This is a kind of beef rib casserole. The beef is seasoned as it is in *kalbi,* then simmered with carrots, mushrooms, chestnuts and potatoes.
- **Kim** Most expatriates learn to love this seaweed, sometimes wrapped around vegetables and seasoned rice to make *kim bap,* a common food to take on picnics.
- **Mandoo** These small dumplings filled with tasty vegetables and meat originated in China. They are served in a hot soup *(man doo gook),* fried *(goon man doo)* or steamed *(jjin man doo).* There are special shops that serve only *man doo* and *kimchee.*
- **Naeng Myun** This summer dish, whose name means 'cold noodles', consists of cold buckwheat noodles in cold beef broth. Strips of beef, half a hard-boiled egg and/or vegetables are included. Since many small eateries are not careful about sanitation, many Koreans will eat this only at a reputable place.
- **Yak Gwa** A fried biscuit made of honey, ginger, sesame oil and pine nuts. It is orange or brown and shaped like a flower.

Non-Korean Foods

There is a wide variety of ethnic restaurants in Korea, the most popular being those serving Chinese food, which is different from Chinese food in other countries. Many Chinese restaurants will deliver food to your home, and they are among the most inexpensive restaurants in Korea. There are a number of elegant, rather expensive Chinese restaurants as well, and these are of exceptional quality.

Red peppers, an important ingredient of many Korean foods, drying on a straw mat.

The Japanese occupation left many imprints on Korea, one of them being food. Most Koreans enjoy a variety of Japanese dishes, and there are numerous, somewhat expensive restaurants serving Japanese foods.

First class hotels offer delectable Western foods, but you do need to pay for quality. One popular, though expensive, recent development is the buffet, which serves delicious Western, Korean and Chinese food for one set price.

Note to Expats

The fiery red peppers and strange vegetables may scare a new arrival. Start out slowly, trying those that appeal to you. When you grow more accustomed to the food, you can be more adventurous in your cooking. Eating is surely one of the pleasures of living in Korea.

Being invited to someone's home for a meal or out to eat at a restaurant is truly an honour. Most Koreans are aware of Westerners' fears about Korean food, and they are sure to have food that you like. The Korean manner of communal eating is particularly convenient for the reluctant eater: each person takes as much or as little as he wants. The host's main concern is that you enjoy yourself, so eat whatever you want, and do not be concerned about not being brave enough to try the little fish with edible eyes. Keep in mind that a good host provides far more food than can be eaten and that it is polite to leave food in the serving dishes.

Eating at a low table, sitting on soft cushions set on the *ondol* floor is the most gracious way to eat in homes and restaurants. In homes it is usually done in the master bedroom. Men traditionally sit cross-legged, women sit with knees bent and legs together, to one side. If you get uncomfortable, stretch your legs straight in front of you under the table.

HOLIDAYS

Koreans work hard, but they also play hard. While many of their vacations might not be considered relaxing, they are a break from everyday routine. Since many Koreans do not own cars, express buses and trains are common ways to travel. Their happy spirit is able to overcome all the hardships of carrying luggage and/or children from bus, to train, to bus, and to hotel.

For many working Koreans, July 15 to August 15 is vacation time. This is also the time when children have their school holidays, and generally when the city heat is at its most intense. Consequently, there is a mass exodus from the city and all the vacation spots are packed.

If, to avoid the crush, an expatriate wisely plans a vacation before or after this time, Koreans will be sure to say he should not go swimming because the water will be too cold. On August 15 the beaches will be crowded but by August 20 there will be few Koreans in sight. If people-watching is your goal, by all means go during the month-long vacation period. Do not, however, count on peace and relaxation.

The Old Vacationers

Perhaps because elderly Koreans take public transport, or because they often travel in large groups, it seems that the proportionately few

124

Cultural performances are an important part of many vacations.

elderly people living in Korea take more than a fair share of vacations. These groups are easily spotted by their light-coloured traditional clothes.

They have amazing energy, always travel in groups of all men or all women, and tend to spend their time sightseeing. They particularly like vacationing at mountains or hot springs. After a lifetime of following the strict etiquette of Korean society, they are finally free to do as they wish. This may include staring at and talking about an expatriate.

Segregated Travellers

Traditionally, men took their holidays in groups of men, with no women. For some, this is still the preferred way to spend a vacation, and one still sees such groups, generally extremely noisy, though now there are societal pressures to spend time with their families. As one might guess, such vacations are spent sightseeing, drinking and gambling, with very little time spent sleeping.

Only the wealthy Korean women, who have time to leave their family responsibilities, can travel. It is fun to see such groups as they drop many of the inhibitions of proper Korean ladies.

Students

University students have two two-month vacations every year. They make the most of this time, among other things mountain climbing at Mt. Sorak or Mt. Chiri, enjoying the beaches along the eastern and southern coasts, and visiting the temples scattered throughout Korea.

Groups of students from the same club will holiday together; they call it 'MT' (membership training). When high school friends take a trip together, their enthusiasm carries on through the night, and discos at popular tourist spots are filled with eager youngsters. Often they do not sleep for nights on end, and rarely would anyone sleep more than five hours a night. These trips are seen as a good opportunity to bond relationships.

Family Vacations

In a country where, traditionally, contact between the sexes was forbidden after the age of five, families vacationing together is a new phenomenon. The women often encourage this kind of vacation simply because it means they get to go too. Children welcome any chance to get out of the normal routine.

The destinations are often chosen with the children in mind. One is struck by how little the parents talk to each other, and how the father seems to be on the fringes of the group. No wonder most men, especially those over 40, prefer to take trips with their friends.

Note to Expats

If you are part of a Korean group, they may invite you to accompany them on a vacation, with or without your family. This is a sign of closeness and a desire to get to know you better. Chances are you will enjoy yourself, but do not expect it to be relaxing.

For a country as small as Korea, there are an amazing number of scenic, historical and enjoyable places to visit. Driving through the country itself can be relaxing. Some of the more popular vacation spots include Cheju Island, Mt. Sorak, and the eastern and southern coasts. Decent hotels may be found at the many natural hot springs, including one called Bugok Hawaii in the southeast and Onyang Hot Springs a few hours south of Seoul.

TRADITIONAL FOLK GAMES

Department stores and the *moon bang goo* (a kind of Korean stationery store) sell modern toys and games, but these are newcomers to the Korean home. Most Koreans over 40 had few if any toys when they were children. Still, they had lots of fun, as many do even today, playing traditional Korean games such as *yoot, paduk, changgi* and *nul ddwee gee.*

Yoot

This game is particularly popular on New Year's Day. There are four sticks, rounded on one side and flat on the other. The players are divided into two teams, and take turns throwing the sticks into the air. If they land with one side flat and three round, one point is awarded the team. If the result is two flat, two round, two points. Three points are given for three flat and one round and four points for all flat. The maximum of five points is given to the team with all rounded sides up. The teams advance a marker around a circle, and the first team to finish wins.

Part of the fun in playing this game is the yelling and cheering. Every time the sticks are thrown, one team or another offers loud encouragement. The food and alcohol thoughtfully provided by the hostess add to the fun and noise level. When this game is played, it does not go unnoticed by neighbours.

As Koreans find it hard to explain the game to the foreigner, they are likely to encourage him to throw the sticks just like the other players. No matter what the result, they will tell him he has great skill, and he is likely to believe them, not knowing exactly what skill is required. In any case, it is a lot of fun for people of all ages.

Paduk

This game, called *go* in Japan, is especially popular among men. It is played on a wooden board that has squares drawn on it. Small markers are placed at the intersections of the lines. One player has black markers, the other white. The goal of the game is to surround the other player's pieces. Strategies to achieve the object can be very complex and many educated people spend hours each week playing *paduk*. Games played by nationally recognised players are sometimes televised.

Paduk requires great concentration and a lot of time. For some reason, it is played particularly often at estate agents' offices.

Changgi

This game is similar to chess. Each player has 16 pieces, of 7 different types. They are placed on a board with 10 horizontal and 9 vertical lines. The player who immobilises his opponent's pieces wins the game. *Changgi* is especially popular among working class people. The board and pieces are made in a variety of sizes, and portable versions are often taken along on picnics.

Nul Ddwee Gee

This Korean see-saw is different from Western see-saws, and is particularly popular among women. A long board is balanced on a bag filled with rice straw. The participants stand on each end. One jumps into the air and lands on the board, sending the other flying. It takes skill to time a jump to coordinate with a partner's landing.

The game was especially popular during the Yi dynasty, when women were confined inside the high walls surrounding their property. As they leaped high into the air, they hoped to catch a glimpse of the outside world. It was also a good form of exercise, for women could not get out for any.

One is not likely to see this game played much in cities, but at the Folk Village, south of Seoul, visitors may try the *nul ddwee gee*.

Kite Flying

On the lunar New Year, which often falls in February, boys like to fly kites. Korean kites are usually white with a design of red, blue and yellow painted on them, and they very often have a large hole in the middle. They are flown by holding the string wrapped around a reel made with four sticks.

Sometimes the fliers glue glass dust on the string, and try to approach other kites in mid-air in order to cut their strings. Traditionally, on the last day of the first moon, people would write 'Away Evil, Come Blessings' on their kites and release them, fondly believing that their families' bad luck would fly away with the kite.

Kite flying and jumping on the see-saw are two traditional folk games still enjoyed today.

Swinging

The Korean swing was traditionally used primarily by women. The swing was hung from a tall tree or a special stand by thick ropes. Players would stand up on the swing. This was an especially popular game during holidays. Expatriates can also try this at the Folk Village at Suwon, to the south of Seoul.

Shi-reum

Shi-reum is a unique form of Korean wrestling. Each participant binds his right leg tightly with a long cloth. He grabs his opponent's thigh with his right hand, and the end of the cloth with his left hand, then the participants face each other in a semi-squatting position. To win, one player must force the other to lose his balance so that his body touches the ground. This game is always played in a sand pit.

– Chapter Six –

INTERACTING WITH KOREANS

How well one adjusts to Korean life depends greatly upon how well one gets along with Koreans. It is important to understand that Korean rules are different from yours, and equally important to realise that patience and good humour will take you a long way, as will a general knowledge of Korean culture and customs.

Koreans are quick to forgive foreigners their mistakes. You can avoid making many by heeding some specific advice for interacting with Koreans in particular settings.

Introductions take on a special meaning in a society where rules of etiquette apply only to those you have properly met. (You may recall from a previous chapter that people you have not met do not exist.) The Korean way of introducing people is discussed below. Some general information about conversation is given, as well as advice on interacting with Korean officials, socialising in public, and being entertained in a Korean home. Special tips are supplied for your own entertaining, for dealing with other people at home, for shopping, and for getting along with taxi drivers.

KOREAN OFFICIALS

It will appear to the expatriate that he has more contact with government officers, policemen and various other people in positions of authority than he would ever have had in his home country. One particular difficulty in this kind of interaction is achieving the correct balance between giving enough respect (so as not to offend) and giving too much respect (thus lowering one's own position).

Where possible, have someone else interact with the officials, as it is time-consuming, and many officials do not know much about working with expatriates. Some companies in Korea have staff experienced in helping foreign employees in these matters. Drivers seem to be very good at going to Immigration, or explaining to local police who resides at your home. If there is someone to run such errands for you, you should pay transport costs, as well as a little extra (about 10,000 won) for their trouble. Eventually, however, you will have to make contact with an official on your own.

The Middleman at the Desk

The first person you see rarely has any authority. He is a screen before the various layers of decision makers. If you are upset about something and complain to the man at the desk, he probably cannot do anything to help you. He has to follow his boss's orders exactly, even if they are irrational. So when he appears weak and unconcerned, remember that his position as middleman is probably the most difficult job in the office.

Flexibility

Rules, like many things in Korea, are flexible. In fact, laws are often written broadly, to be interpreted by the individual officer, the one with power in a particular office, not the middleman you first meet.

If you want the official to be somewhat flexible in your case, by all means ask. You may even request to speak to the supervisor, but this will prejudice any future interactions with the man at the front. A nice smile, a few Korean words, and a polite attitude can go a long way, or can get you nowhere at all. Never mind the lack of logic in these encounters. Just remember: you will have to put up with them anyway, so why not keep them pleasant?

Note to Expats

Most expatriates have had the experience of being asked to come back again with some additional information, only to be told, when they do, that one more document is required. Why they could not be told about the two missing documents at the same time is a mystery with no solution.

Immigration

As a non-Korean citizen, everything you do is subject to approval by the immigration authorities. In recent years they have become quite strict, monitoring foreigners' activities carefully. Doing work that has not been specifically approved in advance can result in a fine or even imprisonment. Many expatriates, however, do part time private work such as teaching English to housewives or tutoring students. Such work is generally not reported.

INTRODUCTIONS

Introductions are not taken lightly in Korea. In many Western countries, if two people happen to be at the same place at the same time with a mutual friend, the latter will casually introduce them. In Korea, an introduction (*So gae*) permanently changes the way two people relate to each other in the future. Introducing a person of relatively little status to someone of higher status is uncommon.

Before two people meet for the first time, their mutual friend will probably give both some background information on the person they are about to meet. When they actually meet, there is a ritual which is invariably followed. If one person is sitting when another (standing) is to be introduced, the former will stand up. This is true of women and of men. One person will say something like 'This is my first time to see you.' The other will make a similar statement. They will then face each other directly, bow and say their names. '*Cho eum boeb ket seum ni da*' is the Korean for 'How do you do'*; 'Man na byoe-o pan kahp seum ni da*' is 'I am glad to meet you'.

It is sometimes difficult to hear the names as they are bowing, but that does not matter as, following the bow, business cards are exchanged. This gives both a better idea of their status in relation to each other. Men often shake hands at this point, sometimes extending two hands to show respect for the other person.

Knowing a person's status is critical, since the proper language level to be used depends on the two people's positions. Until they know, they will both use very formal, respectful language.

Once introduced, they can talk. Much of the early conversation will consist of personal questions, seeking some connection that will make them feel closer. If their names are the same, they will ask for the origin of the name. For example, if the two people turn out to be the same 'Kim' (such as Kimhae Kim, meaning one's early ancestors came from the city of Kimhae), they will quickly warm to each other. Other common factors sought are previous schools attended, home town and hobbies. If one person is obviously older than the other, he will begin addressing the younger in more intimate language.

Rarely do Koreans introduce themselves to someone with whom they have no connection. It does sometimes happen that two people strike up a conversation, perhaps sitting next to each other on a long bus ride, or when a query leads to a longer conversation. Before they part, one will say 'I guess we don't know one another's names.' They will then say their names, bow and exchange cards. A future relationship will have been established.

Note to Expats

Never forget the importance of introductions. Though you may feel uncomfortable not introducing your wife or a friend who is with you when you chance upon a colleague on the street, it is better not to burden your colleague with an introduction. Also, do not ask to be introduced to someone unless you have a particular reason to want to know him.

It goes without saying that you must never run out of name cards which state your name, company and exact title. If possible, have the information written in Korean on one side of your card. Have a system for organising other people's name cards for your easy reference. Once you have been introduced, you can call and ask for assistance of any kind.

Koreans place their family names before their given names, but when introducing themselves to foreigners, they often follow the Western custom of placing the family name after the given name.

CONVERSATION

Many Koreans like to talk to foreigners. Some, especially those who have travelled abroad, will approach an expatriate, eager to make him or her feel comfortable. But most Koreans are reserved compared to Westerners. Some are embarrassed by their poor language skills, and some just do not know what to make of a stranger, especially one from a strange land.

Personal Questions

In getting to know one another, Koreans will often ask quite personal questions. It is usual to ask someone if he or she is married, and if not, why not? If married, for how long? If no children, why not?

Except for much older women, asking someone their age is not considered impolite. If your clothes are a bit different from Korean clothes, you can expect questions about them. Such questions are not intended to embarass you, and most of them would be asked of Koreans and non-Koreans alike.

There is no obligation to answer questions if you are not so inclined. Your conversation partner's primary concern is usually that you feel comfortable. If you consider a question too personal, answer humorously and change the subject, or pretend that you didn't hear. Try not to let on if you feel offended.

Small Talk

As you have probably guessed, personal questions can be suitable small talk when interacting with Koreans. You can ask for details of someone's job, but be sensitive if he wishes to reveal only basic facts. Koreans often ask about hobbies, and you can do the same. Men enjoy talking about their military experiences (nearly all men serve for two or three years). Women can be asked about their children. People who have travelled find it interesting to compare travel stories. As most Koreans are well-read about national and international events, current news can be discussed.

Koreans are very eager to hear your opinion about anything Korean. They are very pleased to hear which foods you like, what places you have visited in Korea, how Korea favourably compares to other places you have lived, and how kind and polite Koreans are. Such statements, if sincere, are sure to increase the *kibun* of any Korean.

Sensitive Topics

Some personal subjects are not acceptable for discussion. One is income. (But do not be surprised if you are asked what you earn; some rules applied to Koreans will not be applied to you!) Sex-related topics are never discussed in mixed company, and only among close friends of the same sex. Koreans are probably quite interested in your opinion about Korean politics, but they are often reluctant to offer their own.

Koreans will not talk much about their families, especially if there has been some trouble or a death. Anything related to adoption or being the child of a second wife is strictly taboo. It used to be bad manners to say anything good about one's wife or children, and though this is changing, Koreans are still modest on the issue.

Koreans are sensitive to your feelings about a subject, and you would be wise to be equally sensitive to theirs. If they do not wish to discuss something, they may smile at your question and say nothing. Or they may appear uncomfortable and try to change the subject.

To many expatriates, it seems that Koreans are particularly sensitive to criticism of Korea. You will be asked hundreds of times about your first impression of Korea, and how you like living here. Strongly negative comments will not be taken well. Criticism should be gentle and sandwiched between compliments. Koreans are proud of their heritage and their country. Anyone bold enough to judge these negatively would not be viewed favourably.

Conversations between Men and Women

At most social gatherings, the men and women quickly divide. In a home, men will go to one room and women to another, probably the kitchen. Korean men often think women's thoughts too trivial and uninteresting; some think that women do not have the ability to understand complex ideas. Women lead quite different lives from their husbands and they may find male conversation boring. Quite apart from all this, some of the Confucian thinking behind segregating the sexes after the age of five continues. It is often awkward and strange for them to talk together.

Expatriates have a little freedom to step beyond the realm of unspoken Korean regulations, but it is generally best to follow the Korean custom. If an expatriate man spends too much time talking to

137

a Korean woman, people may silently find fault with him. Some Korean men may be eager to talk to foreign women, especially if their husbands are not with them, but other people may get the wrong idea. Some expatriate women find that few Korean women can speak their language; when such is the case, staying by their husband's side may be acceptable.

SOCIALISING IN PUBLIC

Social relationships being as important as they are in Korea, it should come as no surprise that Koreans spend a lot of time entertaining and being entertained. Spending time with other people also means a good break from some of the fatigue, frustration and stress of daily life. There is a variety of places and ways to do this.

Coffee Shops (Tea Rooms)

If you went to a different coffee shop (also called a tea room) every day for five years, you still would not have visited every coffee shop in Seoul. One is almost always within walking distance of a coffee shop. Some specialise in a particular kind of music, such as classical or pop. Others emphasise atmosphere: clean and modern, quaint and homey, or bright and bold. Many employ a disc jockey who sits in a small booth and announces different songs, occasionally accepting requests written on small pieces of paper. Coffee shops generally serve coffee, tea, fruit juice and other non-alcoholic drinks.

Their primary purpose is to provide a place for people to meet. With traffic and other unpredictable events, it is hard to get anywhere at a specific time. But coffee shops are comfortable places to wait for friends, read and sometimes socialise with a waitress who is not too busy. Some people go to a coffee shop to be alone, to escape the pressures of work or school for a moment. Others go there to spend hours talking with friends. There is no pressure to leave when you have drunk your coffee, and coffee shops remain open until late in the evening.

Friends and business acquaintances often start after-office social-ising at a coffee shop. Then, after an evening of fun, they will end up in another coffee shop, enjoying another fragrant cup. Once you have grown accustomed to Korean coffee shops, it will be hard to find a place in your home country that fulfils the same purpose.

The Café (Kyong-yang Shick)

Cafés are a cut above coffee shops. People also use them for relaxing, meeting other people and getting quick refreshment in the middle of a cold winter night or a sizzling summer day. Their atmosphere tends to be more sophisticated, more romantic and cosier. A Korean man who wants to impress a woman would probably take her to a café rather than a coffee shop. Of course, for the classier mood, one must pay a bit more.

The biggest difference, however, is not the atmosphere, for the ambience of some coffee shops can rival that of many cafés. Cafés, unlike coffee shops, serve food and alcohol. They often have steaks, pork cutlets, spaghetti and pizza. Also, very often, they have a few inexpensive Korean entrées, such as fried rice or curry rice. Cafés tend to be located near universities or in fashionable shopping and business districts.

Garden Restaurants

There are a growing number of restaurants that serve traditional Korean food outdoors – weather permitting – or in semi-outdoor settings. Expatriates appreciate this type of restaurant, and for good reason: the food is generally quite good and the atmosphere is pleasant. Some are well landscaped, with a waterfall near the tables, and others have the traditional Korean swing.

Korean food barbecued at your table seems to taste even better when cooked outdoors, and the smoke rises into the air instead of circulating in the room. Alcohol is usually served.

Some major hotel restaurants include traditional dance performances to enhance the pleasure of a meal.

Hotel Restaurants

Perhaps because hotels are so similar worldwide, or because non-Korean travellers are numerous among hotel guests, expatriates generally feel quite at home at hotel restaurants. They are taken to hotel restaurants quite often and they choose to do some of their own entertaining there as well. The service is good and the facilities spotless. There are often special features, such as a strawberry festival in spring, or a buffet featuring a special theme, perhaps the food of one foreign country. There are many hotel restaurants to choose from, and the English language newspapers advertise some of their special attractions.

Drinking Holes

Much has already been written about the important Korean drinking customs (see Chapter Five). Sometimes drinking is accompanied by a meal at a restaurant. At other times, it is after a meal, at a beer house, bar or *salon,* where food may also be served with the alcohol.

Beer Houses

There are many beer houses *(saeng maekjoo chip)* in Seoul and in other cities throughout Korea. These places are generally small, and not as clean as coffee shops or some restaurants. They are nevertheless well patronised by college students and the middle-aged. Beer houses serve draft beer and usually sell appetisers and fried chicken which goes by a strangely familiar name, *ken tuck key chee ken*!

Bars

In Korea, these are called 'stand bars' and they are quite nice. Appetisers *(anjoo)* are served. Sometimes there is a stage and people can sing their favourite songs in front of the audience. At other stand bars professional singers or comedians perform. When a show is in progress, it is noisy and difficult to converse. Few women will be seen at these bars.

Salons

Salons are more expensive drinking places than bars or beer houses and you may need to make a reservation in advance. Each party has a private room. There is usually a live band or a simple four-piece orchestra that plays on a stage or goes to individual rooms.

When people visit a *salon,* they are expected to have the company of women as they drink. The women are often better educated than those who work at other drinking holes, and they expect to receive a generous tip. One hostess is present for each man. She pours drinks and chats with her 'partner'. The pleasant atmosphere of *salons* makes them a good place to conduct difficult business negotiations.

Dancing Places

Dancing has gained popularity in Korea in recent years. In the dancing places, a variety of which are located throughout the country, foreigners may be surprised to find men dancing with other men, and women with other women. In Korea, this is quite normal.

It is easier to meet new people at discos and nightclubs than at other eating and drinking places in Korea. Men can ask women they do not know to dance.

At both discos and nightclubs the payment system is the same. A group of people will pay for a table. That price includes a set number of bottles of beer, and a set amount of *anjoo*. If two people go, they will have a lot to eat and drink, but it will be expensive. For four or five people, the reverse is true. Nightclubs are generally more expensive than discos.

Discos

These are particularly popular with the younger set, but older people frequent them as well. Some discos still feature live bands, but with increasing labour costs, many now have sound systems instead. Itaewon, the famous shopping district for foreigners, becomes a hot disco spot at night, for expatriates as well as Korean nationals.

Nightclubs

Some nightclubs are located in hotels, others stand alone or as part of a building. They usually have a live band and dancing, and some employ women to act as dancing partners for patrons.

Who Pays?

In Korea the rule is quite simple: the person who invites pays. Even among close friends, it is considered impolite to 'go Dutch'. Anyone close enough to eat a meal with someone would certainly be willing and eager to pay for the meal. Among Korean men and women, there seems to be a kind of unspoken calculation so that all people end up treating each other an equal amount.

Tipping

Tips are not expected in Korea. Guests should be treated kindly because they are guests, and not in the expectation of tips. Hotels do add a 10% service charge and a 10% tax on to their bill. The money paid to hostesses who accompany customers is also called a tip, but it is often set in advance. It is not necessary to tip anywhere else.

Toilets in Public Places

One is not, of course, expected to socialise in washrooms, but it is quite likely that you will need to use them when you socialise in public places. Korean toilets may surprise foreigners.

Naturally, standards vary greatly. Toilets in hotels and many of the nicer restaurants closely resemble those one would find in a Western country. Remember that if someone knocks on your toilet door to see if it is occupied, you simply knock back to indicate your presence.

Some toilets are used by both men and women. Men's urinals are lined up against the wall as you enter the room. Then behind or to one side are the individual booths. Expatriate women are sometimes uncomfortable walking past a man who is relieving himself. Cleaning women feel no shame, and get on with it, no matter what goes on. It takes a while to get used to this arrangement, but most foreigners eventually do.

A surprise greets the foreign woman when she enters some booths. There is a strange-looking toilet at ground level, and she is expected to squat over it. It is more difficult to use if she wears trousers. Unless there is a cord to pull, flushing is done by the foot. The handle close to the floor is not meant to be touched by hand.

HOME ENTERTAINING, KOREAN STYLE

Guests hold a special place in Korean society. Special food is always prepared for a visitor and no expense is considered too great. The main concern of host and hostess is that you enjoy yourself, eat well and feel comfortable.

Invitations

Last-minute invitations are the norm. If you think it is hard to drop everything and go, imagine the poor hostess who has to shop and cook for 20 on a few hours' notice.

Traditionally, women did not accompany their husbands to social functions. These days they are sometimes included, though the invitation, even if it is written, probably will not mention the fact. If you ask your host, he will say that of course your wife is included, but she may then turn out to be the only female guest. It is best to ask another person who has also been invited. If no one else has been invited, you have no choice but to ask the host. Children are rarely included in such invitations.

To show respect to host and hostess, you should dress decently, men in tie and suit, women in a dress (not trousers).

Arriving

People are often invited in a group. It is usual for the guests to arrange to gather at one spot, then proceed to their host's home. This is particularly true when no spouses are included. Sometimes meeting together first is done to help those who do not know the way. It does make it more convenient for the host.

Do not worry if you are unable to arrive at the specified time. Arriving 10 to 15 minutes late is all right, but being more than 30 minutes late is insulting. Never arrive early, however, as it causes some embarrassment.

Koreans greet their guests at the entrances to their homes. As they do not wear shoes indoors, you should remove yours at the door. Expatriate women have learnt to wear slip-on shoes, but the men cannot get around the awkward tying and untying of laces. (They should remember to check their socks for holes, however; walking around all evening in holey socks can be embarrassing.)

Sometimes, as you enter the house, you will observe slippers set out for guests. If the floor is cold, these will provide insulation.

Slippers are also a protection from unpleasant falls on slippery wooden Korean floors. You may choose not to wear them.

Gifts

Visiting empty-handed is impolite. The usual gift is a box or bag of fruit, bought at the local fruit stand. A gift from a bakery or florist's is also appropriate. For a host who enjoys his glass, alcohol makes an excellent gift, particularly if it is a foreign brand. Gift-wrapped boxes of fruit juice make suitable gifts and if there is a child, a small toy would be well-received.

Inappropriate gifts are money, towels and decorative items for the home, with the exception of any kind of gift representative of your home country or city. Do not bring a gift in your own container, such as home-made cookies on a plate, as your hostess will then feel obligated to fill the container before returning it to you.

Pot luck dinners have not caught on in Korea, so do not bring or offer to bring any part of the meal.

The Meal

Guests invited to a Korean home are invariably served a meal. Sometimes drinks or fruit juice and an appetiser will be served in the living room, but most meals will be given in the master bedroom, called the *anbang*. Being invited into the master bedroom is an honour.

A low table will be set in the master bedroom. If there are many guests, several low tables will be placed end to end. Seating is on large, soft cushions. The whole meal will be served at one time, with rice and soup beside individual plates and all side dishes spread out in the centre.

Before the meal, the host or hostess often says 'We do not have much to eat, but please eat a lot.' It reflects the Korean attitude that even the biggest feast is not good enough for their guests.

Before the meal, conversation is amicable, but when the main

145

course is taken, talking is unusual, as people are focusing completely on the delicious food. The host or hostess will encourage you to eat and will be pleased to see you enjoy yourself. This is again a Korean expression of concern. You may be obliged to eat more than you wish.

Koreans usually do not praise the food, especially in the presence of the hostess, the way many Westerners do. Be assured, however, that compliments will be well received.

After the Meal

As soon as the main meal is over, coffee is served with cut fruit. By this time, the male guests should be loosening up with the effects of alcohol, and talk will be quite pleasant.

If you are the most honoured guest, you will soon be asked to sing. This is a sincere request, so prepare a song ahead of time. Pleading a poor voice is not an acceptable excuse. Often, as one sings, the others will clap or join in.

Leaving

Singing and drinking can continue for several hours. The longer guests stay, the more assured the host that they are enjoying themselves. When the guests are ready to leave, the host and hostess will accompany them to the door.

After guests have put on their shoes, they face the host and hostess, bow and say goodbye. Sometimes the host will accompany them to the front gate, in which case the bowing takes place there.

ENTERTAINING KOREANS AT YOUR HOME

Koreans are very pleased to be invited to someone's home. They sincerely appreciate any effort you make to treat them kindly, to feed them or make them comfortable. Any blunders will be overlooked. Here are a few tips from experienced expatriates to help your entertaining go smoothly.

Invitations

While Koreans who have lived in other countries are accustomed to formal, written invitations, in Korea people are usually invited informally, with little advance notice, sometimes only a few hours before the event. Most expatriate wives would prefer to give a little notice, but invitations given more than a week in advance may be forgotten.

It is only recently that Korean women began accompanying their husbands to some social functions. Some Korean men and women are still uncomfortable about doing this, so even when you invite women, they may not come. You will probably not be notified of this in advance.

Though you may ask your guests to come at a particular time, they may be a little late. In unusual cases, they may arrive up to an hour late. It is important to have a flexible menu, bearing in mind the possible delay in serving time.

Greetings

It is a Korean custom to greet guests as they arrive. Even if you are in the middle of something important, drop everything and go to the entrance to welcome your guests. The hostess will graciously accept any gift, then return to her work while the host makes the guests comfortable.

Drinks and Appetisers

Guests should be served some food and drink from a tray as soon as they arrive. It is better to use an unopened bottle of liquor as this gives the impression that you bought the alcohol just for them. The host should pour drinks for his guests in their presence. The hostess should never do the pouring; in the Korean context this is done only by bar hostesses and would make Koreans feel uncomfortable.

While you can ask guests for their choice of drink, they may not answer you, or they may say they do not want anything. Refusing is considered polite. You should give them something anyhow. Female guests may be given alcohol, but do not expect them to drink much.

It is appropriate to serve a wide variety of appetisers. Korean appetisers or *anjoo* are readily available, and please everyone. They include dried fish, dried meat, nuts, raisins and roasted seaweed. Biscuits and chips are not considered elegant. Some non-Korean appetisers that are well received are Japanese *sushi,* devilled eggs and oysters. Cheese is popular among Korean children, but is not eaten by many adults.

The Dinner Menu

Be prepared to serve a banquet: your Korean guests deserve special food. Not only should the quality be excellent, but there should be an ample amount for everyone. Koreans may feel insulted or unwelcome if they are served what they consider to be only a few items.

With the exception of those who have travelled abroad, many Koreans are apprehensive about eating non-Korean food. They are delighted, however, if you hire someone to prepare the meal, Korean-style. Whoever you hire to prepare the food will probably know what to prepare. Serving beef is important; pork or chicken alone would be insulting. Koreans usually serve *bulgogi* or *kalbi. Chop chae* is always popular, and a fish or chicken dish would go down well with Koreans. There must also be numerous other side dishes, and never forget the rice, soup and *kimchee!*

If you think your guests would prefer to eat Western food, an imported ham might be a good main course. Steaks or any other beef dishes would also be enjoyed. Most Western vegetables, on the other hand, are tasteless to Koreans, but a particularly spicy vegetable dish should please them. Most Koreans also enjoy breads.

Many expatriate wives have discovered that a combination of Korean and non-Korean food works best. That way, timid eaters can stick to the Korean food, which the hired help can prepare. A few speciality dishes from your own country would then add an exotic flavour to the meal. Even if the guests do not know what to make of your spinach soufflé, they will appreciate the trouble you have taken for them.

Serving the Meal

While many first-rate hotels in Korea serve expensive and elegant buffets, people generally do not serve buffet-style in their homes. Being served at a table is more gracious. Since expatriates' homes are usually not set up in the Korean style, service at a Western table is more convenient.

If Korean food is being served, chopsticks should be provided. Even expatriates feel that it is strange to eat *kimchee* with a fork! Any kind of table setting will work, but a nice one would be appreciated.

Alcohol may be served throughout the meal, and care should be taken to refill empty glasses. Other beverages are usually not drunk until after the meal. Koreans themselves serve water at the end of the meal. It may be easiest to place a glass of water beside each plate at the beginning of the meal.

There is no need to assign places. People will naturally sit down where they feel comfortable. Guests will probably sit near people of the same sex.

Dessert

Koreans always appreciate fruit after their meal, no matter how full they are. Fruit such as apples, peaches and pears should be peeled, cut to bite-size pieces and attractively arranged on serving plates with tiny forks. Coffee or tea would be appropriate at the same time.

If you enjoy making desserts, you can serve home-baked items in small pieces with the fruit. Koreans generally would not serve sweets after a meal, but they would almost certainly be very appreciative of any you prepare.

After the Meal

If you have urged your guests to eat more than they intended, you have succeeded in being a good host. After the meal your guests will most likely continue to eat and talk. Make sure there is always some kind of food available for them to eat. Taking all the food away conveys an impolite message: that it is time for them to depart.

At a Korean party, people would start to sing, but they may feel inhibited in an expatriate's home. If you enjoy this custom, you could encourage the most honoured guest to begin the 'recital'.

Bidding Guests Farewell

Korean guests will leave your house at the same time. As the host and hostess, you should accompany them to the door. It would be even more thoughtful to escort them to your gate or to the area outside your apartment. According to Korean custom, a host or hostess who bids their guests goodbye from inside the house is insulting them. Having said goodbye properly, you can then relax inside your suddenly quiet home, knowing that if any mistakes were inadvertently made, they will be forgiven.

OTHER PEOPLE IN YOUR HOME

When culture shock is at its height, the place you will long for to escape from this confusing and seemingly hostile society is your own home. Supposedly, there you can be in control, feel relaxed, and follow the customs of your own country.

Unfortunately, no matter how similar your home is to the one you left behind, you will be unable to keep elements of this strange culture from seeping through.

Maids

Most foreigners find that the only way to keep their sanity is to hire a maid to do some of the tasks that took only minutes at home but seem to take hours in Korea. In fact, for many women, having a maid is reason enough to live in Korea. The house is kept cleaner than you've ever kept one yourself, and your little children receive constant loving attention, leaving you free to enjoy various aspects of Korea. Besides, most Korean maids are adept at preparing delicious food.

The price of household help, however, has increased in recent years. Consult other expatriates for an appropriate wage. For busy people it is still worthwhile to hire a maid, at least for a few days per week.

But convenient as maids are, there are a number of potential problems you should try to avoid.

Hiring a Maid

The best way to find a maid is to get one from an expatriate who is leaving the country. Foreigners often try to find their loyal maids new homes before they themselves leave Korea. Get in touch with other expatriates. If no one can refer a maid to you, there are several agencies in larger cities that train their own maids, some of whom can speak your native language and who are familiar with Western customs.

Interview a maid before you hire her. Check that her language ability is satisfactory. It is very difficult to find one who speaks well, but the more simple directions she understands, the easier it will be for both of you to adjust to each other.

Probably even more important than language is whether you feel comfortable with her. This will be evident almost immediately. Does she show you a proper degree of respect? Is she cheerful, talkative, silent, passive, neat, and generally to your liking? This person will be in your home, and if you are not comfortable with her, your adjustment to Korea will be much harder.

Once you have decided to hire someone, agree on how much you will pay, when you will pay (daily, weekly or monthly) and what bonuses will be paid. Usually one full month's bonus is given at Chusok or New Year (either January 1 or the lunar New Year, see Chapter Four), or both. If you are hiring more than one person, make sure they understand who you consider to be the one in charge. Talk about what happens if the maid is sick.

Her First Day

If you have never had a maid before, you will think it is wonderful when she sweeps the floor or hangs out a load of clothes to dry. Many new expatriates feel uncomfortable having another person doing all their unpleasant tasks for them. This feeling will not last long. As culture shock sets in, the maid may easily become a target for your pent-up feelings.

It is easier to prevent problems than to remedy them later. Explain to your maid what you want her to do. Demonstrate exactly how you want it done, paying particular attention to matters of sanitation. Korean methods and standards are quite different from Western ones, and you will probably want it done your way.

She will try hard to please you in every way. At first it may seem considerate of her, but after a while it will drive you crazy. You have to remember the system of the society you now live in. Koreans are rank-oriented; Koreans are subject to the whims of their seniors; and Koreans of high status seem to like having several people within earshot to perform any task on demand. It is natural, for instance, for your Korean maid to wash a spoon as soon as you finish using it. It is your responsibility, if you feel confined by such behaviour, to let your maid know that you would rather she did her own work, and that you would do yours without her constant assistance.

It is important to distinguish between a maid and a friend. She is not the best person to listen to your complaints, nor does she need to know about your marital difficulties or your son's progress in school. You are clearly of higher status, and it is best you operate in that mode.

Helping Your Maid Feel at Home

Even the maid who has worked in an expatriate home before may think your behaviour quite strange. She may be unsure of how she should act, and be timid about asking you any questions. Sometimes you will have to anticipate what she might want to ask.

You will also need to encourage her to take care of herself. She may not take a break unless you insist. And she may stay up late into the night, trying to finish all her work. Be sensitive to her food preferences. Some maids enjoy Western food, while others have difficulty eating it. At first, she may feel uncomfortable helping herself to anything.

Cleaning

Some of the biggest problems expatriates have had with their maids are related to cleaning. Korea was a poor country until recently and your maid would be among the Koreans who have not received the trickling down of wealth. Some of her cleaning methods are due to poverty (not being able to afford oil to heat the dishwater, for example), and some are cultural. As old habits die hard, unless she has worked with other expatriates, it is unlikely that she can make the transition to your own standard of sanitation easily.

Most Koreans wash and rinse dishes in cold water. They put a generous amount of soap on a washing rag, rub it over the dish, rinse it in cold water, and set it aside to dry. Of course, unless your home is very dry, it stays wet, but this does not seem to matter. Putting away a wet plate and using it wet at the next meal is felt to be quite all right.

A pan used for frying anything, from an omelette to *bulgogi* and fish, is never washed. This makes sense when you do not use hot water since it would not get clean anyhow. But most expatriates are bothered by a greasy pan sitting around, and do not want six meals in a row cooked in the same unwashed pan.

Clothes may also be cleaned in a way that seems strange to you. Until recently, Korean washing machines were not very effective and few people owned one. Clothes were, and often are still, either washed vigorously on a scrubbing board or beaten with a special bat. To be sure, this method gets clothes extremely clean. It also wears them out very quickly. Your thick cotton towels will be noticeably thinner after a few 'treatments'. Once shown the wonders of an effective washing machine, though, many maids are pleased to give up the exhausting hand washing.

Bathrooms

Korean bathrooms were traditionally located outdoors and not considered part of the house. They often smelt, and a dirty bathroom was inevitable. In many homes, this is still the case.

Bathroom floors are rarely dry. The bathtub is for storing water, as not too many years ago water shortages were common. When many Koreans bathe at home, they stand on the bathroom floor and spray the shower nozzle over themselves. All Korean bathrooms have a drain in the floor for this purpose. A pair of rubber shoes is kept inside every bathroom, so that the feet do not get wet whenever one steps inside.

A bathroom is usually cleaned by splashing water over the mirror, sink and floor. If you have a rug on a tiled bathroom floor, you can imagine what might happen to it if you did not give your maid special instructions. You will have to demonstrate in detail how you want the bath, floor, sink and toilet cleaned.

Giving Orders

Some expatriates have difficulty giving orders to their maids. Many coming from a Western background do not really like to give specific orders, preferring to explain the general duties, and expecting the maid to use her own initiative.

Many Korean maids have trouble following general instructions. They are good at washing the dishes and going to the market for some vegetables according to your wishes, but 'taking care of things' when you are not there is much harder.

Then there is the reverse case, of maids, particularly those older than yourself, who think they know more about what you want than you do. (This can also be true of other people in Korea.) You have a

154

right to expect things to be done your way, within reason. In some cases, a Korean friend's clear explanation in Korean is all that is needed. If a maid's contrariness persists, it is best to look for a new one.

Drivers

Many expatriates in Korea employ drivers. Indeed, with all the other culture shock, who needs to deal with Korean streets? Women have found drivers very handy with odd jobs around the house: they can hammer in some nails, rescue a cat out of a tree, or repair a bicycle. They can also be expected to run errands.

Many of the comments about maids apply to drivers as well. One needs to feel comfortable with them. The more of your language they know, the easier it will be. Duties, pay and working hours should be spelled out in advance. Keep an appropriate distance from them, for they are neither relatives nor friends.

Gardeners

Expatriates with gardens are likely to employ gardeners to work for a few days each week. Generally, a gardener will keep any garden in lovely shape without being told what to do. If you have some specific instructions concerning the garden, feel free to say so.

Guards

In Korea, few people would dream of ever leaving their houses unattended. One expatriate stepped outside to pick up some things at a nearby market. Ten minutes later, she discovered her house had been burgled. The police were called and it took them only a minute to discover the culprit – herself! To leave one's house empty is an open invitation.

A maid can occupy your house in your absence during the day, and even at night if she lives in. But for more protection, some homes employ a night guard. He supposedly stays awake, looking out for unwanted guests. Most guards do not look fierce, so perhaps their presence alone keeps most thieves away.

All apartment complexes also retain guards. Their salary is very low, and their job not particularly interesting. It is appropriate therefore to give them small gifts on Chusok and the New Years. This ensures their careful attention in the event that you need it.

Callers at the Door

Answering the door at your home in Korea is reason enough to employ a maid. An amazing number of book salesmen, plant sellers, cosmetics salesgirls, church members and local officials manage to make it to your home. Even if you speak some Korean, you are unlikely to understand exactly what they want.

There is also some danger in answering the door. It is a good way for thieves briefly to scan your home for valuables, or even force themselves into your home. Most Koreans refuse to open the door for anyone they do not know and it would be wise for you to do the same. Your maid will be good at sending away people who you do not want to see.

Related to this are people delivering newspapers. There are two English language newspapers in Korea, and most expatriates subscribe to one of them. However, the other paper, or even a different person selling the same paper, is likely to solicit your business. This is how they may do it: every day for a month they will deliver the unrequested paper, then at the end of the month they will come to collect payment. These people do speak English and will acknowledge the misunderstanding, but would like you to pay anyhow. If you do, they are sure to do the same the following month. This also happens to Korean housewives regularly. Some people pay the small monthly subscription to get the man to leave. But they may continue to have the same problem.

IN THE MARKET

Shopping for groceries will be one of your more enjoyable activities in Korea and pretty soon you will find better quality and lower prices than you would as mere tourists. There are numerous markets, indoor and outdoor, that sell everything from silk and custom-made clothes to door knobs, fresh fish and vegetables.

Your first visit to one of the larger markets may be overwhelming. You will no doubt get pushed around and sometimes nearly knocked down. There are sights, smells and sounds that will stay with you long after you leave Korea. Merchandise does not seem to be arranged in any organised fashion, and food is not as sanitary as you might wish. There is no room for cars, so all your wandering will be on foot. As there are also no shopping trolleys, it would be wise to take a comfortable shopping bag on such an adventure.

The Sellers

People selling things are among the lowest in terms of Korea's social structure. Perhaps that is why they are so relaxed and easy-going and care little for what others think of them. In Seoul's East Gate Market and South Gate Market, a surprisingly large number of them speak some English, and enjoy practising with you. The shopkeepers are usually friendly and helpful to expatriates. They are also intent on selling anything and everything.

Bargaining

In Korea, department stores and chain supermarkets always have fixed prices. Smaller, individually owned stores and booths generally expect shoppers to bargain. The price of any commodity at the market depends on who is selling it, who is buying, the time of day, the weather, and an equal number of unknown and seemingly unrelated factors.

When you bargain, the first thing to do is to express modest interest in the article. Look it over critically for flaws. Then ask the price. The seller will always tell you a price higher than the one he or she is willing to accept, because by lowering it, you will appear to have been given a favour.

Offer to pay somewhere between half and 75% of the first price. Korean buyers are careful to study the reaction of the seller to their counter offer. If the seller is not shocked, they advise, then you should lower your offer. In any case, you will probably be told that your offer is below cost, then be given another offer, somewhere in the region between your offer and the seller's. You can take it if it seems reasonable, or continue bargaining. Or you can walk away. The seller may take your highest offer as you leave.

It is sensible to look around at various shops or booths to have a general idea of how much a particular item costs. This puts you in a better position to bargain. However, if you have allowed a shopkeeper to go to a great deal of trouble to find what you want, you should not leave without buying something. This is especially true if the shop-keeper has gone to another store to obtain the item you requested, as is frequently done.

Many expatriates who speak Korean are angered when they discover that they have been asked to pay up to three times as much as a Korean customer at the same booth. The seller reasons that, being a foreigner, you can afford to pay the higher price. No doubt, if it means losing a sale otherwise, the seller will give you, too, that lower price.

Loyalty in the Market

One way to guarantee that you get fair prices is to go to the same person all the time. The first few times you may be overcharged but when the seller realises that you are a regular customer, you will be given a fair price up front. This is especially true at food markets, where extensive bargaining does not lower the price much anyhow.

Be careful, though, always to go to the same seller. If you change to the seller next door, because her strawberries look bigger, 'your'

A shopkeeper and customer discuss the price of peppers.

lady will not be so eager to give you her lowest price the next time. If you want something that is not available at your usual shop or stand, let your seller know. She can probably get it from another shop within a few minutes.

Getting used to Bargaining

At first, many expatriates wonder why the prices cannot be fixed. Bargaining takes so much time, and it seems inherently unfair, especially to the foreigner. But after several months of bargaining, it gets to be fun. And there is some logic to it. Suppose you go to a department store and cannot really afford the price of a particular item; perhaps you would buy it at a lower price. By being inflexible, the store loses your custom and you lose the item. Nobody wins. Upon returning to their home countries, some Westerners rediscover the urge to bargain. They feel confined by the inflexibility of their more advanced economies.

Another advantage of bargaining is that it adds a social element to economic transfers: bargaining is a game that creates a relationship between two people, and this is often missing when one buys from uninterested clerks in spotless department stores. Moreover, bargaining brings a sense of satisfaction. Being able to lower a price is a skill, and the more experience you have, the better you get. Some expatriates think of bargaining as a hobby and derive much pleasure from it.

IN A TAXI

Taxis in Korea are noticeably smaller than those in many Western countries. They are usually brightly painted. A sign on the roof reading 'TAXI' distinguishes them from other cars. At night, if a taxi is unoccupied, the sign will be lit, making it especially visible.

Taxi rides in Korea are quite cheap, and guaranteed to be interesting. They also might be the cause of your first episode of culture shock.

Catching a Taxi

It used to be easy to catch a taxi in Seoul, but this has become increasingly difficult with the addition of 300 cars each day to the city's overflowing streets. Some expatriates consider transport to be the biggest frustration of life in Korea.

While taxis can be hailed from anywhere, there are places throughout most big cities with sheltered or unsheltered taxi stands. These force hirers to stay in line, and are a convenient place to let passengers off and pick up others. If there is a taxi stand nearby, the drivers tend to pass over those not queuing at the stand. In a stand or not, you hail a taxi by extending your arm parallel to the street and waving your hand inwards.

Snatching a vacant taxi seems to bring out the worst in some people. There are many taxi tales. One expatriate remembers waiting several minutes for a taxi in the middle of a cold January, holding a small baby. Finally, one drew up, but before she could open the door, a young man appeared from nowhere, jumped in through another door and was driven off. He had obviously seen her, but felt sure that his need should be met before hers. This situation is not uncommon. Sadly, you will find yourself joining this unattractive group of taxi-grabbers. The alternative is waiting more than an hour, or until the rush hour ends. 'Stealing' taxis does not feel right to people raised in queuing societies.

Communicating with the Driver

Some expatriates naively think that because Seoul hosts many international events, all taxi drivers can speak English. English is as difficult for the Korean taxi driver to learn as Korean is for the expatriate, and since he rarely has a chance to speak English, one cannot blame him for not making the huge effort. However, there are radio shows and special free programmes for 'taxi English' and it is surprising how many can actually say a few things in a language so different from their own.

Once you get into a taxi, the driver may or may not ask you, in English or Korean, where you want to go. There are many ways for him to say it in Korean, so rather than learning them, you can assume that anything he says has that general meaning. You respond by giving the name of your destination. If it is a common place, such as Hotel Shilla, or Itaewon, he will have no problems. It is another story, however, if your destination is less common, or if your pronunciation is quite different from a Korean's.

Unfortunately, he often will not respond when you name your destination. This is a cultural behaviour pattern, not directed at you, the foreigner. If you think he is going the wrong way, and you cannot speak Korean, the most you can do is repeat the destination, in the hope he understands you the second time. The chances are he did understand but is going by a route that is not familiar to you.

A solution is to have your destination written down in Korean *(hangul)*. Someone in a coffee shop or your hotel will assist you. Even better would be to give him a road map featuring your destination. However, if it is an obscure place, such as your house, he may well not even understand a map written in Korean. Be assured, however, that most Korean taxi drivers take pains to understand, even stopping to ask people on the street.

The Taxi Ride

Once you are in the taxi, you can have an interesting discussion with the driver. Taxi drivers spend most of their days conversing with passengers, and are one of the best gauges of what Koreans think about any given topic. Of course your conversation with them is limited by the amount of Korean you speak or understand, and by the driver's English.

Most drivers ask simple questions such as 'Where are you from?' and 'How old are you?' in English. They may not understand your answer, and you can answer truthfully, playfully, or not at all. They are only being friendly. If you do not feel like talking, simply do not respond to their comments; they will get the message. Conversely, you should be sensitive to their moods; there are times when even taxi drivers tire of conversation.

If you can speak a little Korean, a taxi is one of the best places to practise it. The drivers are usually quite good-humoured and appreciate any effort you make. And if you make a fool of yourself, you can take comfort in the knowledge that you are unlikely to see them again.

Reaching the Wrong Destination

The times when taxi drivers intentionally go the long way around are extremely rare: they are among the more honest 'strangers' you are likely to meet in Korea. If it happens to you, first assume that it is an honest mistake. This is not easy when you are missing an important meeting, or if you are picking up a friend at the airport and the taxi driver thought you said 'haircut' instead and took you to an exotic barber on the other side of town. Try to remember that the mistake may be as frustrating for the driver as it is for you.

Some taxi drivers will force you to get out in such situations, or when lost. You should do as they say, because they are not likely to do any better the second time round. Perhaps you will find a bystander who speaks your native language and is eager to help you. Otherwise you will have to try another taxi.

Every expatriate and most Koreans would ask themselves why the driver agreed in the first place if he was unsure of the destination. The answer is related to the instinctive confidence many Koreans have about being able to do anything.

A final note on being driven to the wrong destination. No matter how angry you are, try not to show it to the driver. This is for the benefit of other expatriates. Like it or not, most of them must use taxis. Some taxi drivers who have suffered a bad experience refuse to pick up foreign passengers. So, no matter what the destination, pay the fare registered on the meter, smile and try to believe the best.

Wild Driving

Korean taxi drivers are known for their wild driving. Several years ago, the fare was determined solely by how many kilometres they drove. Cynics said that once the fare was also calculated on how long the ride took, they would slow down. The fare system has changed but it has made little difference.

Most expatriates find their first taxi rides a terrifying experience. The driver seems compelled to move forward as fast as possible, and it does not matter that he has to slam on the brakes only a second later. In fact, these men are skilled drivers and escape close calls hourly. They know the corners of their cars to the centimetre and appear to enjoy brushing within two centimetres of other cars.

Taxi drivers frequently work long hours for below-average pay. Sometimes their driving habits reflect this.

New arrivals should take heart from the fact that while all expatriates felt the same when they first came to Korea, they are still riding in taxis. And they rarely even shudder as their taxi weaves back and forth between lanes.

The Taxi Fare

The basic rate set by the government for the first few kilometres is 1000 won for a company taxi and 3000 won for a private taxi. After that the fare is determined primarily by the distance. If the car is moving very slowly, or waiting in a traffic jam, the meter will also calculate an additional charge. If the taxi goes through a tunnel, the driver will pay the tunnel fee of 100 won which will be added to the taxi fare.

An exception to this method of calculating the fare is when one takes a taxi to another city an hour or more away. Then the fee should be agreed upon before the ride. Also, if the ride is after midnight, the driver is entitled to charge more.

Koreans usually do not tip taxi drivers. Some foreigners do tip regularly and if a driver puts himself out for you, a tip is not out of place. A reasonable tip would be between 500 and 1000 won.

Changing Time, Mealtime

Be warned that around three or four in the afternoon you will find hundreds of taxis whizzing by, but very few stopping. This is the time when drivers of all the more than 100 taxi companies change shift. Drivers will only pick up passengers going in the direction of their garages.

Lines at taxi stands lengthen during this time. Taxis pull up to the stand and wait for everyone to yell out their destination. If none of them is the right one, they simply drive on.

When an empty taxi goes past you, with the driver making a strange motion towards his mouth, it simply means he is breaking for a meal. It is thoughtful of him to let you know, but frustrating nonetheless.

Hapsung

Two strangers may share a taxi in a *hapsung* arrangement. Taxi drivers, having already picked up one passenger, stop by every potential passenger, hoping to pick up one more going in the same direction. Two passengers mean double the fare.

Hapsung is illegal because it interferes with traffic. While the driver is trying to pick up passengers, he weaves his car in and out of the right-hand lane. One passenger also has to wait while the driver takes the other to a slightly different location. It is widely practised, however, especially during the rush hour. The more people riding *hapsung,* the easier it is for the others to catch a taxi, and the overburdened taxi driver will have the chance to make a little extra money. You may also be lucky (or unlucky, depending on your viewpoint) enough to ride with someone who speaks your language. However, if your driver spends a lot of time trying to find another passenger going in your direction, you have the right to complain.

If you decide you want to try *hapsung* when there are no vacant taxis, wait for a taxi to stop, then yell out your destination. If the driver is going your way, he will motion for you to get in. If not, no one expects him to waste any time; he will just drive on.

Your fare should not change just because he is taking a longer route to drop someone else off. There is no way of calculating this exactly. If you are sure he is taking a longer way, pay as much as it usually costs you, or estimate, though he may not agree with you. Sometimes the taxi driver will charge you less because of the inconvenience caused as a result of *hapsung.*

– Chapter Seven –

DOING BUSINESS IN KOREA

In 1961, South Korea's per capita gross national product stood at only US $82, one of the lowest in the world. This densely populated country with few natural resources was just beginning to rebuild itself after the Korean War. In 1996, the per capita GNP was about US $11,4000, a remarkable increase in just 35 years. Since 1996, the Asian financial crisis dealt a severe blow to Korea. Fortunately, Korea has been able to rebound from that economic hardship quickly.

A combination of factors fostered this economic miracle:
- the discipline instilled by Confucianism
- a highly literate population
- native intelligence
- a strong desire to achieve

The Korean working week is the longest in the world. What has been labelled the 'Korean work ethic' is clearly evident to anyone working with Koreans.

Along with the phenomenal economic growth and a massive drive to export everything from sweaters and shoes to television sets, computers and automobiles, is a move towards international business. This accounts for the increasing number of expatriates sent to Korea to conduct business.

Doing business is not easy even in one's own country, where most people speak a common language, where communication generally follows standard rules and where the word 'contract' is understood by all. It becomes a hotbed of frustration in a country where the same language and rules do not apply.

The purpose of this chapter is not to help you set up a business in Korea: there are government agencies that do this. It is to help you with the cultural aspects of doing business Korean style. Information is provided to help you avoid some of the likely pitfalls in Korea, as well as giving you an understanding of how businesses in Korea operate. A short reference section on business do's and don'ts may be found at the end of the chapter.

BUSINESS RELATIONSHIPS

Westerners are known for their efficient, logical approach to doing business. While Koreans also want a profitable business, they place great importance on the people conducting the business and on the nature of their relationship. By Western standards, this stress on interpersonal relationships is excessive.

Agreements, proposals and contracts are all made in the context of the people doing the business. If a potential business partner does not appear trustworthy, no matter how good the deal looks on paper, the contract is of little value. In other words, feeling comfortable with and having positive vibes about a business partner takes precedence over profit in Korea. Often, before any business discussion can begin,

A talented small businessman in Korea, hand-crafting drums which are widely used in Korean folk festivals.

two potential partners must meet for dinner and drinks. Only after a few drinks, when they have an insight into one another's characters, can they begin to think about doing business together.

Along this line of thought, it is much easier to do business with a person with whom one has a connection, whether this connection is the old school tie, the same home town, or a mutual friend. That link inclines two people to treat each other more favourably in business.

Koreans believe that conducting a business relationship within the context of a social relationship is both safe and humane. To them, considering a business in purely profit-maximising terms ignores the fact that people, not computers, are conducting the business. They wish to be treated as individuals, and they are likely to view you as such. And where does the individual stand?

Position

Korean society is based on a hierarchical social system in which Koreans need to know the position of another person in order to determine how to relate with him, whether in terms of respect given or the language to use in conversation. Korean business is part of this social system.

Titles

Individual identities are closely tied to the positions they hold within a given organisation. For this reason, knowing the position of a Korean businessman is significant when one interacts with him.

A clue to the importance of position lies in the way Koreans address each other. They would never call President Kim, plain Mr Kim. Nor would they use his personal name. Managing Director Park is addressed as such, never as Mr Park or by his personal name. Koreans are familiar with the Western way of calling people by their personal names, or by the usual honorarium of 'Mr', as in Mr Smith, instead of Director Smith. But they would appreciate the effort to call them as they call each other – by their titles.

169

Actually, using the title not only gives each Korean his due respect, it helps the foreigner distinguish between the multitude of Mr Kims, Mr Parks and Mr Lees!

Dealings with People of Other Rank

Presidents, supervisors and managers tend to have more power over their subordinates than they might have in a similar Western organisation. So ingrained is Confucian respect for seniors, that it is difficult for a Korean to criticise or go against what his senior thinks or wants. Those occupying lower positions have little choice but to follow their seniors' directions.

Presidents, especially those in larger organisations, have learnt to delegate responsibility. So while it is nice to be introduced to people in high positions, they will sometimes know little about your particular project, and will refer you to the appropriate person. Presidents and supervisors will often trust dependable subordinates, so it is important not to offend or neglect the lower ranks.

Generally, people of similar positions in different organisations work with one another. If you have a high position in your organisation, and a person of noticeably lower status acts as the representative of his company when relating to you, you can assume that the company is not particularly interested in what yours has to offer.

COMMUNICATION

Communicating effectively is a prerequisite to conducting a successful business in any country. It is also one of the most difficult skills to master when doing business in Korea.

Introductions

In Korea, when you wish to begin a business relationship with someone, it is very important to be introduced to that person by a third party. Contacting an unknown person directly without going through an intermediary is viewed with suspicion.

In view of the significance of introductions, it is easy to see why you should maintain as wide a social network as possible. Fortunately, since South Korea is a small society, it is not as difficult as you might think to be introduced to persons you wish to meet. Alumni can also freely contact each other, even though they have not been formally introduced, as can members of the same social or business association.

If you know who you wish to approach, you can ask the people you do know to introduce you to that person. Even when they are unable to help you, they will probably introduce you to someone else who can, in turn, introduce you.

Language

The good news is that, with only a few exceptions, English is the language of business in Korea. This puts people from English-speaking countries at a clear advantage, especially as Koreans are familiar with the various accents of English-speaking nations.

The bad news is that there are still plenty of barriers to good verbal communication. While all educated Koreans have studied English in middle school, high school and college, many have had little, if any, experience communicating verbally: the emphasis has been on reading and writing. Until recently, speaking and listening skills, so different from those used in reading and writing, have not been taught. Many Koreans may have difficulty understanding you and expressing their own ideas in English.

At first, you may be deceived by their apparent English-speaking ability into believing that their oral comprehension ability is equally good. No one will enlighten you as to how much is understood: they may be too embarrassed to show how little they know. You can help by doing the following:

- Speaking patiently and slowly.
- Repeating key points several times, or even writing them down.
- If speaking to two Koreans, pausing from time to time so that one

may translate for the other, or to allow them to discuss with each other (in Korean) what they think you are saying.

- Finding a tactful way of asking the listener to paraphrase what you said.

Many experienced business expatriates in Korea stress the importance of learning some Korean. This will endear you to your Korean partners. It is probably unrealistic to expect anyone who plans to live in Korea for two to three years to learn to speak the language fluently; it is sensible, however, to learn several useful expressions.

The Meaning of 'Yes'

In English, 'yes' usually means 'I agree' or 'I will do it'. The Korean 'yes' means 'I understand' or 'I'll do my best'. It is important you understand exactly what someone means by his 'yes'.

Recognising the Korean 'No'

This impolite (to the Korean) word is seldom heard in the Korean business world. A Korean would say no indirectly. A Korean banker put it thus: 'Rather than saying I won't make a loan, I make the loan conditions so unfavourable that it could not possibly be accepted.'

Sometimes a Korean may agree to do something, but later you find it is not done. His intention is not to deceive you. He may have meant, 'If it is possible, I will do it', then later discovered he could not. When a promise to do something keeps being put off, he may be indirectly saying 'no'.

Use of the Telephone

Business communication by telephone is not the norm in Korea. The telephone is used to make appointments, or to confirm small points, but most business communication occurs face to face. Direct personal contact also tends to strengthen the personal relationship between the two parties.

Nonverbal Communication

Besides the nonverbal ways of communicating discussed in Chapter Two (page 49), there are a few that refer particularly to business people in Korea.

It is essential to dress your part in Korea. The clothes you wear reflect your status, and they show a certain amount of respect to the person you are conducting business with. A tie is always necessary, and when you leave the office a suit jacket should be worn.

At the office you are likely to hear people talking more loudly than you would at an office in your home country, especially when they are talking on the telephone. Some expatriates have linked this louder talk to former days when the telephone service was bad. In any case, do not be surprised when one of your shy secretaries answers the telephone with a powerful voice.

You may also encounter difficulty in correctly interpreting a Korean's smile. Besides being an expression of happiness, a smile can mean shame or embarrassment. When your assistant mistakenly erases several hours of your work on the computer, he is most likely to smile, or even laugh. This does not mean that he finds the situation funny. It means that he is embarrassed and sorry. You will quickly learn to read the smile by the particular context.

TIME

The large conglomerates which deal extensively with foreign countries are very prompt about appointments, orders and contracts, but there are a number of medium and small companies that operate on a more 'flexible' sense of time. Many expatriates find it frustrating to accept the relaxed standards, but we wish to point out here that Koreans are noticeably more prompt than those in some other newly developed countries.

It was not long ago that Korea was primarily an agricultural society. Time was more flexible, but things got done, sooner or later. Following a strict schedule was not critical. The country has moved away from that concept of time, but remnants of the old way of thinking remain.

Deadlines

When a Korean agrees to do something within a time frame, he generally says 'about this time'. This gives all parties concerned some leniency in case the unexpected happens. When a contract is written up, an exact deadline may be stated, but the Korean will assume the same flexibility exists as in a verbal agreement. After all, the two parties trust each other, and each must assume that the other party will do his best. Only a reason beyond his control would prevent a person from meeting a deadline.

Showing anger in the face of a late order is, in effect, to doubt the good intentions of the responsible party.

Appointments

Getting anywhere on time in Korea is fraught with hazards. Traffic, running into a friend, or an important phone call can all interfere with appointments.

Koreans understand that being up to 30 minutes late is no cause for concern, but to a Westerner such a delay is serious indeed. Koreans know this, and usually make a special effort to be prompt when dealing with expatriates. The expatriate who shows he is upset over an unexpected delay would not, however, be looked upon favourably.

Another source of frustration for the expatriate is the time it takes to complete a project. Some socialisation is necessary before one can even discuss business. Various people need to look over a contract before it is signed, and they do not make it their first priority. Or a long Korean holiday comes up, during which no work can be done. Be prepared to allow much more time than you would think is necessary to complete any business process.

CONTRACTS

While contracts often form the basis of business deals in South Korea as in the West, the nature of such agreements is often significantly different.

When a Contract Isn't a Contract

Misunderstandings often arise over the issue of contracts. Most of the large international South Korean companies have learnt the meaning of contracts, sometimes after being sued. Many smaller companies are still in the dark about contracts.

The problem is that Koreans and Westerners view contracts differently. To some Koreans, a contract is merely a general guide for conducting business. A change of conditions, some Koreans assume, may invalidate the details of a particular contract. Anyway, a contract is not as important as the interpersonal relationship between the two parties. One made between two people who do not trust each other has little value.

Fortunately, an increasing number of Koreans now recognise that contracts are legally binding. It is necessary, though, to be aware of the other view of contracts.

Reaching Agreement

The politeness and gentleness that many Korean businessmen exhibit may fool you into thinking them pushovers in the negotiating process. Actually, Koreans lead very competitive lives, beginning in elementary school, through the university entrance examination, right up to competing for a position in their company. They hold their own at the negotiating table.

You will need to be firm about your position, remembering two things: insisting on having your way, with no flexibility, will be viewed unfavourably by your Korean counterparts; and appearing to be in a hurry puts you at a disadvantage. Being flexible does not imply giving in to demands that you consider totally unreasonable.

Koreans prefer to reach a general agreement, leaving sticky details to be worked out later, perhaps by subordinates in the two companies. In fact, they would prefer not to be too specific in the contract, but to allow flexibility for both parties. Often, contracts are made verbally, in a social context, and written up formally in the office later.

Once the contract has been written up, it may take time to get the final approval. Sometimes several government agencies need to be involved, each with its own process of red tape.

LOYALTY

Patterns of loyalty in a business context in South Korea vary from those in Western countries.

Loyalty to People

In Korea, people are employed, transferred and promoted on the basis of who they know. For this reason, personal connections are usually more important than ability. The best way to move up is to be completely loyal to someone 'on the rise', because when he finally has the power to fill positions, he will look to those who have been loyal to him. He would generally choose a loyal person over a more competent but unknown person.

Koreans are not particularly loyal to business organisations. If a better opportunity comes up, moving to another company is natural. If one has been particularly loyal to a higher-positioned person in one's own company, when he is transferred, he may very well try to open a position for his follower. It is a comfortable arrangement: he is happier having a loyal person working for him, and his follower sees it as his just reward for being faithful.

Loyalty to Companies

When you do major business with one business group in South Korea, you should do most of your smaller contracting through them, too. If you shop around to get the best price, you may be viewed as disloyal and your business dealings will suffer.

Even at the outset, if you approach several different companies about a particular proposal, you may find them all rejecting you. Your behaviour, in their opinion, has not been 'sincere'. Do not imagine your initial inquiries can be kept quite discreet and secret, because these business people meet regularly to socialise and word invariably gets out. It is best to do research about the various companies beforehand, and then concentrate on the one that appears most useful to you.

BUSINESS MANNER

As a foreigner, you will not be expected to follow Korean etiquette to the letter. But there are a few differences you would do well to remember.

Respect

The company president deserves complete respect. His needs and desires come before any other aspect of the business. He expects his employees to be ready and willing to assist him at any time, in any way.

If you are the president of a company, you can expect your employees to revere you in this manner. When you arrive in the morning, they will all rise to acknowledge your presence. They will also probably not leave the office until you do, even if they have no work, and even when you stay very late. Leaving before one's boss is considered disloyal. To a lesser extent, this is true for the subordinates of supervisors, managers, and other people in authority.

If you work for a Korean president, he probably will not expect you to follow the Korean rules of behaviour, but you should never forget that his position is higher than yours, and you are not equal in any sense.

Refreshments

Whenever you visit someone's office, you will be served a drink. You will often not be asked beforehand what you would prefer, but it is impolite to refuse what you are offered.

Likewise, when someone comes to your office, you should serve them something. It is not necessary to ask your guests what they want.

Korean secretaries are accustomed to preparing coffee or fruit juice, but some more educated ones may not like serving drinks. If you have this situation, delegate the job to another person in the office; it would not be proper for you to make or serve refreshments.

Gifts

Gifts are a common way of showing appreciation, or getting someone to view you more favourably. They are sometimes given during important Korean holidays, such as the New Year (most commonly in the business world on January 1), Chusok or Christmas. If you receive a gift at such times, it is important that you send a reciprocal gift.

Always take a gift whenever you visit a business friend at home. It is sometimes appropriate to do this when visiting the office as well, particularly if you have been abroad recently.

Bribes

What the Westerner may call a bribe is called a gift in Korea. Giving a large sum of money so that someone will view your company more favourably is not frowned upon. Sometimes a gift of money is given after a contract has been made, a sign of appreciation for a particular person's help. It seems somewhat natural in Korea. The details of these 'gifts' (how much, when and whom to give) are far too complicated for the foreign expatriate, and are best left to Korean colleagues.

Entertaining

As in other countries, entertaining is an important part of doing business in Korea. The only difference is the degree to which entertaining seems necessary.

To begin a business relationship with someone, one generally dines and drinks. Then, to solidify the relationship, regular socialising is necessary. During negotiations, drinking and dining can soothe the way for easier discussions. And finally, after a business agreement has been made, regular social contact is advisable, for when inevitable business kinks appear, there will be a relationship of friendship and trust to fall back on to solve problems amicably.

Do not overlook the role of alcohol. Drinking with someone is a sign of trust. Drinking a lot with someone breaks down social barriers quickly. You may be surprised at how much easier business becomes, within and outside your own organisation, after a night of hard drinking.

Much, perhaps even the majority of business, is conducted outside the office. To Koreans, the mood or the social atmosphere (the Korean *kibun*) is extremely important. Therefore, huge amounts of money are spent to create a conducive atmosphere. This always includes outstanding food, plenty of alcohol and often beautiful women. Who would not be more inclined to give in on a minor business point after a beautiful woman whispers how attractive he is?

When you are treated to one of these delightful evenings, it is important that you also invite your host to a similar event. Failing to reciprocate would show you to be greedy. This form of socialising is usually done in groups and includes several people from the businesses concerned.

Chapter Eight

MATERIAL CULTURAL MUSTS

In this chapter, we shall discuss briefly the main areas to look out for in planning your stay in Korea. We cannot provide comprehensive details in a book such as this. Several organisations and books already give excellent up-to-date information about housing, transport, clothing, education and health in Korea. For these references please refer to the Resource Guide at the back of the book.

Here we shall concentrate on living in Seoul. By far the majority of expatriates in Korea live in or near the capital. Some do live happily in other parts of the country, and major cities such as Pusan, Taegu and Kwangju offer similar services and accommodation to Seoul, with perhaps fewer options. Those who live in smaller towns may not find some of the services listed here, but they should not despair: South Korea is a fairly small country, and some of these services are worth a short drive to a major city.

HOUSING

This is probably the most immediate concern of newcomers to South Korea. There is a wide variety of housing options suitable for foreigners, and every year more attractive housing units are being built. The prices of many things in Korea are reasonable, but the price of housing is not. Monthly rents for apartments range from US $2000 for those with one or two bedrooms, to US $6000 for a four- or five-bedroom luxury apartment. Very small houses may be rented for as little as US $4000 a month, and larger houses for up to US $8000 a month.

Choosing an Area to Live In

Some companies find housing for you, and others expect you to live in the home your predecessor lived in. If you can contact your predecessor, you will at least know what the drawbacks are, and may then settle in more quickly.

In most cities, you will notice areas with a high concentration of foreigners. There are obvious advantages to living near other expatriates. It is pleasant to be near others who speak your language and who can give you support and advice. Supermarkets that cater to expatriates' tastes are conveniently located in these areas, softening the effects of a different culture.

In Seoul, apartments that house a large expatriate population include Nam San Apartments, Hyundai Apartments, Hanyang Apartments, Chung Hwa Apartments and Shin Dong Ah Apartments. Houses of expatriates are often found in the UN Village, Hannam-dong, Pyongchang-dong, Songbuk-dong, Itaewon, Dongbinggo-dong, Dongbu Echon-dong, Kangnamdong, Bangbae-dong and Yunhi-dong.

Some housing areas in Seoul are extremely dense.

Help from the Estate Agent

Unfortunately, with very few exceptions, apartment complexes do not have rental offices. Apartments are individually owned, and only a real estate agent can put you in touch with the owner.

Real estate agents tend to specialise in housing for one specific area. So if you can decide where you wish to live, you will know where to find an estate agent. The English-language newspapers advertise some English-speaking agents; they also specialise. The same agent may cover several apartment complexes and housing types in the same area. Agents for one area may also contact agents from other areas to help you find the type of housing you require.

You can walk into any estate agent's office in the area you have selected, or get references from other expatriates. Any estate agent's office displaying English signs probably speaks some English. The agent will make contact with the owner and take you to the apartment or house of your choice.

Once you find a house that you wish to rent, the estate agent will help you agree the contract, and he collects commission from both parties, usually a percentage of the rent. Visit as many estate agents as you like, but only pay the one who took you to the house or apartment you eventually decide to rent.

Systems for Paying Rent

A very few landlords accept rent paid by the month, a method of payment which is convenient for those who might move out of the country with little notice. Most apartments and homes require the whole year's rent in advance, which can be quite a fortune.

Other homes and apartments require only a large 'key money' deposit (US$100,000 upwards), but when you move out, you are refunded the entire amount. Where, you may ask, is the benefit to the owner? In Korea, money lent privately can earn up to 36% interest a year; interest on 'key money' can exceed what the owner might get in rent. Some owners ask for a combination of 'key money' and rent: for example, US $20,000 'key money' plus US $3000 a month.

The Contract

A multitude of problems may crop up after you agree a contract, so you are advised to consult a lawyer before signing one. Clauses covering repairs, utilities, renewal of lease, subleasing and termination should be included. The contract should be made in both English and Korean. FOCUS and The American Chamber of Commerce (see page 238) have detailed information about this subject.

Utilities and Maintenance

Costs for utilities vary considerably between the different types of housing. A three-bedroom apartment might cost US $300 to maintain in the summer and $400 in the winter. A large house might be $700 in the summer, $1000 in the winter. Newer buildings are usually heated more efficiently than older ones in the winter. Houses can cost much more to heat and cool than apartments, but apartments can have high monthly maintenance fees. Some apartments only have hot water during certain hours. Be sure to ask about this if you value your comfort.

Monthly electricity, water and telephone bills will come by post and must be paid in person at any bank. Some companies do this for their expatriate employees.

Getting a telephone installed used to take up to a year and several hundred dollars, but now throughout Korea telephone lines are installed within a few days for a low fee. You will be expected to buy your own telephone instrument.

TRANSPORT

Many expatriates in Korea are provided with a car or buy their own. A car can make life more comfortable. It is also possible to use the excellent public transportation system for some or all of your travel. Expect some adjustment time before you are able to get around easily.

Driving Yourself

If you are used to driving in your home country, you may like the freedom of driving yourself. Many expatriates brave a month of driving before feeling perfectly comfortable with the Korean system.

It is a good idea to get an international driver's licence before coming to Korea. After a few months, you should obtain a Korean licence. This can be done without taking a driving or written test – you simply show your home country licence and prepare some time-consuming forms. Driving is on the right.

Hiring a Driver

If you own a car but do not wish to drive, you will need a driver. If you hold a high position, your company's status would be enhanced by having a driver. Much time and hassle can be saved with one, especially when parking in congested areas. For more information about hiring a driver, see Chapter Six.

The Subway

Seoul is expanding an already large, efficient and convenient subway system. Maps of subway lines are printed in English and obtainable at various tourist facilities. Fares are very reasonable and based on the distance travelled. Though crowded during the rush hour, subway trains have the advantage of not being held up by other traffic. If there is a subway stop near your home, it may be the fastest way to get to many places. The subway is called *Chi Ha Chul* in Korean.

Buses

Seoul is serviced by thousands of buses, and other cities by many bus lines. There is no map of their routes, and as they are run by a multitude of companies, there is no central number to call for information. Except for a few destinations, the routes are never written in English.

Bus fares are low and buses can get you exactly where you want to go, once you know which number to take. Your neighbours can probably help you find the correct bus for your needs. Beware of different coloured bus routes and slight variations on your bus number, for example 148 and 148-1. The routes may be similar but they are not identical all the way.

When the bus is crowded, you may have to remain standing. Remember always to give up your seat for an elderly person.

There is a special commuter bus system in Seoul. The fares on these buses are higher and they can be distinguished easily by their green and cream colours. Commuter buses supposedly operate only when every passenger has a seat. They are more comfortable than the regular buses, with air-conditioning when needed, and make fewer stops, getting you to your destination more quickly. In Korean they are called *chwa soek bus.*

Public transport in Korea is readily available, efficient and inexpensive, but it is not always particularly comfortable.

Taxis

To ride in a taxi, you have to hail one on the street. There is no radio taxi service. The fare is very reasonable, and most times of the day they are easy to find. For more information on how to get along with the taxi driver, see Chapter Six, page 161.

Express Buses

The fastest way to travel outside your city is usually by express bus. They offer air-conditioned comfort and generally travel over smooth express roads. Fares are reasonable, probably costing under 25,000 won for travel between any two cities in Korea. It is possible to buy a ticket a few days in advance, but most people buy them on the spot. Buses leave every ten or fifteen minutes to most cities.

In Seoul, the huge express bus terminal is located in Kang Nam. Once at the terminal, just state your destination and someone is likely to point you in the right direction. There are several different bus companies and the building can be confusing, but sooner or later you will find the point of departure for your bus.

Trains

Most trains leave from the main station of the city. Seoul Station is located just south of City Hall. You may need a Korean guide the first time you travel by train. People with children find trains are the most pleasant way to travel, even though they take a bit longer than express buses or private cars and the fares are higher.

CLOTHING

Clothes worn in Korea are quite similar to those worn in Western countries, although styles tend to be more conservative and a bit more sophisticated than in the West. At the time of the 1988 Olympics one almost never saw shorts being worn outside of one's immediate neighbourhood, but now it seems quite the fashion for younger women and men. To be on the conservative side, expatriates may still want to confine their wearing of shorts to their homes and would not want to wear them to a Korean's home or when Korean guests were expected. It is not uncommon when dropping in at a Korean's home to wait a few minutes before being shown in while the host or hostess quickly changes into more appropriate attire.

Since Korea has four distinct seasons, you will need clothes for the full range of climates. Heavy coats, boots and gloves are necessary in the winter, and Korea's hot, humid summer requires lightweight clothes.

Fortunately, it is possible to buy most articles of clothing in Korea for somewhat less than one would pay back home. This is especially true for smaller people. Children's clothes in particular are reasonably priced, comfortable and adorable. A few shopping areas sell clothes which have been made for export, including larger-sized ones. There is also an abundance of dressmakers and tailors to custom-make your clothes. Some people have a 'sewing lady' visit them once a week to do custom sewing and mending.

Two items expatriates may have more difficulty buying in Korea are underwear and shoes. Koreans require smaller sizes than many Westerners, so the latter are often forced to select from a very limited range. In the case of shoes, there are stores that will custom-make them, but it is still not easy to get a good fit.

EDUCATION

Most expatriates in Korea are very satisfied with the education their children receive. Schools for expatriates tend to be very academic. Finding programmes for special needs children can be difficult. Families often choose a foreign school nearest their home. Schools in Seoul for expatriate children provide a bus service to most areas of the city.

Note to Expats

Most foreigners living in Korea send their children to one of the excellent foreign schools. A few non-Korean families have sent their children to Korean schools, and have been quite satisfied. Expatriate children readily learn the Korean language, and upon returning to Western education, find themselves well ahead of their classmates, especially in mathematics and the sciences. They appear to have no particular problem fitting in with their Korean classmates.

Sending a child to a Korean school requires much forethought, and while a good decision for some, it is not what most expatriates do. Talking to other expatriates who have made this choice would be a necessary step before embarking on it. Refer to the Resource Guide at the back of this book for more information.

Libraries

Many Korean universities allow expatriates to use their libraries. Also, families of foreign students can use their school's library.

BOOKS

There is an increasing number of books available in English about Korea, on topics as diverse as tourism, Korean cuisine and shamanism. Although most are readily available in Korea, it is worthwhile to get hold of a few before you arrive. If they are not available in your country, write to your Korean employer, and ask them to send what seems to be the most useful from the list in the later chapter called Further Reading.

If you are in Korea, there are two good places to purchase such books. One is the **Royal Asiatic Society**, which is in Room 611 of the Christian Broadcasting Building at Chongno 5-ga (Tel 763-9483). They have an extensive selection of books in English about Korea. They also organise interesting tours and informative lectures for expatriates. The other is at the **Kyobo Book Centre**, in the basement of the Kyobo Building, across from the Sejong Cultural Centre in Kwang-whmun. There is a large selection of books in English on various topics, and a smaller selection in English about Korea. Both of these places are located near the stationery shop.

HEALTH

Good health can generally be maintained in Korea by taking a few sensible precautions. Medical and emergency services are available for unexpected upsets.

Water

Most drinking water in Korea is safe, but people rarely drink it directly from the tap. Most expatriates boil their drinking water, or they buy bottled water. Koreans generally drink barley tea *(boli cha)* in place of water. Most restaurants also serve this barley tea when you ask for water.

Food

Some smaller restaurants do not have a high standard of hygiene and it is probably best to avoid such food as raw fish unless you are certain that the restaurant has a spotless reputation. Try to eat hot foods always, as the heat will kill bacteria on dishes that have not been washed too well. Cold noodles *(Naeng Myun)* can result in food poisoning if the dishes are not washed properly.

At home, it is important to wash fruit and vegetables carefully, rinsing them often in water. Because of pesticides and herbicides, Koreans always peel apples and pears before eating them.

Doctors

Most Korean doctors have some knowledge of English, and those who have studied abroad are quite fluent in English, Japanese or German. There are many very well qualified doctors, but it is not always easy to find them. The best way is by word-of-mouth recommendations from friends. FOCUS (see page 238) keeps a list of doctors who work with expatriates.

Most hospitals in Korea have outpatient offices on the ground floor, so if you go to a large hospital you can probably get outpatient care for some medical problems. When your Korean friend says he needs to go to the hospital, he is probably referring to the outpatient offices, not the emergency room.

There are also numerous private clinics, often within walking distance of residential areas. Often visits to these involve no waiting time, and the care is more personal than in hopsitals. Of course the range of services can be quite limited. Usually the clinic sign is written in English, often accompanied by a green cross – the symbol for medical care. While doctors at most clinics usually have some command of English, the staff can rarely communicate in English. There are two clinics versed in English often used by expatriates. These are the International Clinic (Hannam Dong) and the Seoul Diagnostic Medical Clinic (Insa Dong). Call 796-1871 to reach the International Clinic and 732-3030 for the Seoul Diagnostic Medical Clinic.

Pharmacies

There are several pharmacies (called *yak bang*) located in every neighbourhood. To communicate accurately, it is best to have the prescription written on paper, in either English or Korean. Prescriptions are also available at hospitals with outpatient facilities. High quality Korean and imported medication is readily available. Some doctors give their patients medication directly, without telling them what it is.

Dentists

The quality of dental care in Korea is quite good. Dental clinics are readily available in any large city in Korea, and the equipment and procedures are comparable to those in Western countries. People generally get referrals from friends. FOCUS also has a referral list.

ELECTRONIC MAIL

For many people who live far from home, being able to connect electronically will be a high priority. Fortunately, this is possible in Korea. If you are a member of CompuServe, you can hook up in Seoul (call 786-5501). American Online users can gain access numbers by calling AOLGlobalnet at 775-6647 in Seoul and 462-5408 in Pusan. If you will be living in Korea for an extended time, you may want to set up an account with an ISP in Korea. Some possibilities, which are in Hangul but provide gateways to the internet in English, are Hitel

(764-0001, 743-0223), Chollian (790-1522, 797-7555) and Unitel (528-0114).

Of course, the cyberworld changes frequently so it pays to contact FOCUS or talk to people who currently live in Korea and have internet needs similar to yours to help you determine the most appropriate service for you.

MONEY

The unit of Korean currency is won. Coin denominations are W5, W10, W50 and W500. Bank notes are issued in W1000, W5000 and W10,000. Bank checks are drawn for W100,000 and over.

Foreign currency and Korean checks can be converted into Korean won at foreign exchange banks and other authorized moneychangers. The exchange rate is subject to market fluctuations. One U.S. dollar is equivalent to about to W1200 at the time of writing. Major credit cards including VISA, MasterCard, American Express, and Diner's Club are accepted at major hotels, departmental stores and large restaurants.

Banks

Foreigners can open a bank account at most Korean banks and at many foriegn bank branches. Bring a passport and/or an Alien Registration Certificate to the bank when opening an account. ATMs are generally located inside the banks and can be used only during business hours (9.30 a.m. to 4.30 p.m. on weekdays and 9.30 a.m. to 1.30 p.m. on Saturdays). ATMs can also be found at major hotels, departmental stores, subway stations and tourist spots. Internationally recognized ATM cards are accepted. Services are available in 11 languages: Arabic, Chinese, Dutch, English, French, German, Italian, Japanese, Korean, Portuguese and Spanish. Information on ATMs for foreign travelers can be obtained from the website http://www.citibank.com, or call 723-9900/023-9900.

Tax

Value-added tax (VAT) is charged on most goods and services at a standard rate of 10% and is included in the retail price. Hotels charge 10% tax to rooms, meals and other services. This is added to the bill. Information on income tax for expatriates living in Seoul can be found at http://www.kexpat.com/tax5.htm and http://www.metro.seoul.kr/eng/living/index_tax.html.

– Chapter Nine –

CULTURE SHOCK IN KOREA

Culture shock has been defined as a special kind of anxiety and stress experienced by people who enter a culture radically different from their own. Suddenly, the methods one has always used to accomplish particular tasks are not effective. Culture shock is generally experienced during the first six months to a year after entering a new culture. Few people escape this particularly stressful period, regardless of how positive they felt initially about entering the new culture.

This chapter will examine the phenomenon of culture shock in detail, with special reference to how it is experienced in Korea. Additionally, the causes, symptoms and ways to respond to culture shock will be elaborated upon. Finally, ways will be suggested to reduce the stress of culture shock, and to survive the stages as painlessly as possible.

WHAT IS CULTURE SHOCK?

- Culture shock refers to the unique problems people have while they are adjusting to a new culture.
- Culture shock is a psychological situation where one no longer feels in control.
- Culture shock includes two kinds of problems: being confused, anxious and puzzled by the way others behave; and confusing, causing anxiety to, and puzzling others by behaving in one's own way.
- Culture shock originates from the belief that everyone is the same.

Babies are born alike. As they grow older, they absorb ways of doing things to get what they need. A Korean baby learns that by receiving a gift with two hands, he is more likely to get another gift the next time. If a Western baby used two hands, his parents might worry that one hand was not strong enough. Many Western children learn that when they are being scolded they should look the person in the eye. Korean children learn to look down. Western children learn that they should question their parents, teachers and other authorities. Korean children learn that they should gratefully accept what others teach them. The ways humans learn to behave, the cultural rules of different societies, vary considerably.

Upon entering a new culture, a person does not know how to behave. Newcomers in Korea do not know when to bow, or how to pour alcohol for an older person. They do not know how to criticise an employee or how to dress for a special occasion. They do not know how to buy something at the market, or what to do when people pull down a child's trousers to find out the sex of the child. These are among the thousands of instances of cultural behaviour that all Koreans know. It has taken Koreans a lifetime to learn these things, and newcomers cannot expect to learn the Korean ways of thinking and behaving in a few weeks or months.

The Logistical Adjustment

Before exploring the phenomenon of culture shock in greater depth, it is helpful firstly to recognise the things that are going on in newcomers' lives that make existence difficult, even without culture shock. An expatriate arriving in Korea is addressing innumerable complex issues simultaneously. While one is learning the geography of the city, beginning to get a glimpse of office politics, trying to form new relationships, enrolling children in school, getting a residence not only selected and leased but re-papered, carpeted and furnished, one's body is adjusting to a new climate. While one is figuring out how (or if) to hire a maid, get a driver's licence and how to file a lost luggage claim, one is also grieving the loss of a familiar community, friends, favourite restaurants and a comfortable routine. These changes are difficult even for seasoned movers. But each of these adjustments could be multiplied by ten when every detail must be negotiated under a different set of cultural rules.

With all these adjustments taking place simultaneously, one does well just to survive. Making a contribution to the job, learning about the country, pursuing meaningful activities, participating in rewarding friendships or learning the language, expectations that one had when one decided to relocate to Korea, prove impossible, and yet these expectations did not seem unrealistic at the time.

What may seem like culture shock at first is perhaps more accurately labelled 'moving-to-a-new-country shock', with the real bolt of culture shock current coming only after one has completed some of the practical adjustments and has a roof over one's head, has learned how to get across the city to work and has stocked one's pantry. No doubt this early phase is draining, frustrating, and overwhelming and one has certainly had opportunities to interface with a new culture, but it is not culture shock *per se*.

Real culture shock sets in when one has settled in for the long haul. Having adapted more or less to the physical circumstances, one is now in a position to adapt to the cultural circumstances, that is, how Korean people see the world and how they behave, and, perhaps even more to the point, how you see the world and how you will behave in a new cultural environment.

The Unconscious Expectation

Most people moving to Korea have had opportunities to interact with people from other cultures, and know that people's habits and modes of thinking differ. Few people consciously expect everyone to be the same. And yet, when examined carefully, most do operate under the assumption that we are all the same. When your maid opens the wire mesh screens in the windows designed to keep out insects so that she can 'let in the clean air', you may think she is crazy to let the heat out and the bugs in as well. In other words, you expect the maid to think like yourself. When movers struggle to remove their shoes as they carry in a sofa, you may think something is wrong with them because they don't behave in the same way as yourself. When asked to sing solo at a social gathering, you may be uncomfortable and perhaps even angry because such a custom is embarrassing in your own culture. These ways of being, thinking and behaving are only surprising, anxiety-provoking, and confusing because we all unconsciously hold an expectation that others think, feel and act the same as we do. We prefer an advance invitation; why don't they? We're not offended if people wear shoes in our homes; why are they?

The assumption that under normal circumstances all people think and perceive the world in the same way is necessary to carry out our daily lives. If we couldn't expect people to return our handshakes, stop at red lights, recognise our academic degrees, understand what we meant by a gift and thousands of other things we do or see on a daily basis, we could not organise our lives. These expectations, that are so vital to functioning in our own culture, are the basis of culture shock, and at the root of the numerous symptoms which accompany culture shock.

WHEN CULTURE SHOCK SETS IN

Culture shock is a pervasive sense of anxiety, confusion, helplessness, irritation and lack of control resulting from a relocation to a different culture, where the expectations we have of others are not being met. There are a number of symptoms, and most people suffer from several simultaneously. Some symptoms stubbornly remain until you are not only adjusted to the culture, but have come to a new self-identity within that culture. Other symptoms, thankfully, crop up only during particularly difficult times, such as when your overseas boss is making an appearance or when a special holiday occurs. It is important to remember that these reactions are normal reactions to an abnormal situation (most people never live outside their own cultures), and that expecting them will make their intrusion upon your life somewhat easier to tolerate.

Excessive Concern over Cleanliness

Every country has different standards of cleanliness. Koreans are very reluctant to eat anything with their fingers. Neither would they dream of wearing shoes inside a home. Newcomers do not often notice these manifestations of Koreans' extreme concern over cleanliness.

On the other hand, newcomers are often alarmed at the instances where the comparison between Korean and Western standards tilts in favour of hygienic Western practices. Owners of small Korean restaurants may wash their dishes with cold water. Public bathrooms are not always as clean as a Westerner might like. In time, most expatriates learn to overlook such differences, but the newcomer may exaggerate their importance. Some newcomers experiencing culture shock refuse to eat in any Korean restaurant. They may make frequent trips to the doctor, convinced they have contracted an unusual disease.

Feelings of Helplessness and Withdrawal

Expatriates often feel they do not know how to do anything: how to tell the maid to come at nine the next day; where to buy mushrooms; how to find out if a business partner understands what they are saying. During culture shock, all annoyances, big or small, become over-whelming. One might try to escape from everything Korean and try to surround oneself with familiar things and people from home. Of course, avoiding the culture completely is impossible, but for a person who wants to withdraw, those inevitable contacts with Korea can be unusually stressful.

Hopelessness

Some newcomers go through periods of depression. 'How can I ever adjust to orange kitchen cupboards?' 'What's the use in trying to be happy in my miserable situation?' Along with the depression comes an inability to do anything to improve the situation. Suggestions from family or friends all seem hopeless. In some extreme cases, culture shock has led to clinical depression.

Desire for Home and Friends

The need for friends and family is especially acute. People need their own feelings and reactions validated. Some write a multitude of letters. Others feel a vacuum that they have never experienced during previous extended separations from family and friends. Some expatriates develop special worries about particular people in their home country, becoming irrationally afraid that their absence will cause loved ones back home unnecessary pain or inconvenience.

Anxiety, Frustrations and Paranoia

Perhaps no expatriate in Korea is able to avoid these symptoms completely. Small frustrations become unconquerable mountains. Some people feel a constant fear that something terrible will happen. Many feel that Koreans are intentionally causing them problems.

Some new arrivals believe everyone is trying to cheat them, perhaps even harm them.

Irritability

With so many unknowns and frustrations, it is natural that a person experiencing culture shock should readily feel irritated. Every day is filled with situations where one does not know how to act. It irritates one that simple tasks seem impossible to execute. And one becomes particularly sensitive to small irritations when difficulties pile up.

Obstacles that were brushed off in a familiar environment cannot be so easily forgotten in Korea. Deliveries did not always arrive on time at home, for example, but that was never quite so irritating. People tend to forget all the irritable events back home, and blame similar irritations on the new cultural environment.

Physiological Stress Reactions

There is a close connection between one's emotional and physical states. People who are experiencing the frustrations and anxiety of culture shock are often more prone to physical problems than other people.

Many newcomers complain that it takes a long time to get used to the water or food in Korea. And, for some, it does. Emotional stress also brings on allergies, back problems, headaches and digestive problems. Luckily, they go away as soon as the most intense period of culture shock has passed.

A Natural Reaction to Culture Shock

The instinctive way to respond to those situations which cause one to feel helpless, irritated, embarrassed and/or anxious is to withdraw from the situation. When bargaining in a different language is too difficult, it is understandable that one might start using mail-order catalogues from home and forgo the market altogether. When asked to attend yet another drinking party where people pour for one another but never for themselves in a perplexing order, it is tempting to stay at home.

It is possible to learn to avoid as many of the unpleasant situations as possible, surrounding oneself with reminders of home, and people who think and behave in familiar ways. Many cling to the expatriate community in Seoul and fill their lives with events which approximate those in their own countries. Much of the time spent in the expatriate community can be spent criticising the host culture and dreaming about the next trip back home. Such conversations validate one's feelings, but they also tend to solidify one's negative opinions about Korea. And although retreating into familiar territory is protection from the irritation and helplessness an expatriate is liable to feel in Korea, it can begin a pattern of withdrawing which becomes a spiral of retreat. This prevents one from continuing to have experiences which lead to better knowledge and ultimate cultural adjustment.

A tourist can experience the exotic aspects of a foreign culture, become frustrated when people don't behave as expected, and leave, taking with him souvenirs of Korean celadon, antique chests with brass fixtures, stories of the frustrations with immigration, and the pictures of 100-day-old boys without trousers on, showing off their 'peppers'. And longer-term residents can live much the same, interacting very little with Korean people, and understanding very little about how ancient Confucian customs affect current marriages, or what dreams a young adolescent girl in Korea may have. But by following one's natural reaction to withdraw from experiences which set off culture shock, one is precluded from really understanding that people think and behave in different ways.

An Alternative Reaction To Culture Shock

How then does one avoid the cycle of experiencing unpleasant interactions in Korea, which lead to a withdrawal, which leads to less understanding, which leads in turn to more withdrawal, irritation, and increasing frustration?

Since one's expectations that people will act and think like oneself will regularly be unfulfilled, it is not possible to avoid culture shock and its attendant symptoms. But it is possible to view these situations from a different perspective that will contribute to a better understanding of Korean expectations and ultimately to greater comfort and knowledge.

Firstly, it is important to keep in mind that it generally is not the actions *per se*, but our own unfulfilled expectations that bother us. Singing in the shower or along with the car radio isn't threatening to us, but doing that same action in the company of colleagues is. A cancelled class does not upset most people, but when you are not informed in advance of its cancellation (as would happen in most Western countries) it is upsetting. A stranger (albeit a doctor) looking at your child's private parts does not seem intrusive, but a shopkeeper doing the same thing is viewed differently.

Secondly, when feelings of disgust, agitation or anxiety arise, you needs to stand back for a moment and consider why you are experiencing those emotions. Realise that it is because something we had expected to happen does not, or because something we had not expected to happen does. What is bothersome is not what someone else has done (asked you to sing, cancelled a class or pulled down your child's trousers), but our expectations that we should not have to sing, should know about cancellations or have our child seen only by a licensed person. When one is able to analyse the source of the feeling (one's own expectations), those feelings generally dissipate.

Thirdly, you need to believe that the anxiety that comes from not knowing what to do in the numerous situations you find yourself in every day is a natural part of learning about Korea, about your own expectations and about yourself. Such anxiety will only diminish by going to the market without a translator, having dinner at a Korean friend's home, and negotiating a contract, Korean-style. Think of these early anxiety-provoking situations as a necessary vaccination against future anxieties!

There is a variety of traditional performances throughout Korea, one way to appreciate the depth, beauty, and humour in this East Asian nation.

Fourthly, avoid concentrating on the negative emotions such as aggravation, confusion, helplessness and embarrassment, for if you do, you will be prevented from seeing other aspects of the situation and thus gaining knowledge that will be useful for the next related experience. Also, by concentrating on the unpleasantness, you will build up negative expectations with which to view similar experiences in the future.

Having done the above, there will certainly be types of behaviour that, though we can learn to expect, we do not like. For example, though we understand that drinking is a custom with a long tradition in Korea, and that the paid women who may laugh or sing with married men have no intentions of disrupting a marriage, we may still dislike the custom. We may have observed countless such occasions, gained a good deal of knowledge about the custom and become no longer offended by it, but we still cannot accept it for ourselves. This is as it should be. To respect yourself it will be necessary to reject certain aspects of Korea. But those instances will be rare once you have a deep understanding of Korea through personal experience.

CULTURE SHOCK EFFECTS ON DIFFERENT GROUPS

Everyone experiences culture shock in different ways, but particular problems of culture shock recur among specific groups of expatriate people.

Businessmen

Expatriate businessmen residing in Korea find themselves spending an inordinate amount of time at work, partly in order to learn a new job and the Korean ways of doing things. Another part of it is the socialisation demanded of all businessmen in Korea, who have little time for themselves. Yet spending time with the family, and having a break from the stress of business in a new culture, is particularly important while one is experiencing culture shock. More advice on doing business is offered in Chapter Seven.

Spouses of People Transferred to Korea

While the employed person (generally a man) is overwhelmed with his responsibilities at work, his wife is left to cope with settling in her family and herself. A company will often help a foreign employee adjust to his new position, but the wife must find her own feet. She is also the one who has direct and frequent contact with Koreans – the estate agent, curtain maker, market vendors, her maid, and numerous other service persons. Each encounter is fraught with difficulties arising from the differences in speed and quality of service between her home country and Korea.

Another big stress affecting the person at home is just that – being at home. Often, the wife leaves gainful employment in her home country. Adjustment from working outside to working inside a home is never easy, especially when you are in a foreign country and have no ready built social support system. Many try to find full time jobs in Korea, only to come up against the inevitable frustration of Korean immigration laws that make this difficult.

Then there is the unbearable boredom. With a maid to do most of the housework, and with no job of her own, the wife finds she has too much time on her hands. Who can spend 24 hours of the day with the children? And when the working spouse finally gets home from long hours of work plus business socialising, he would rather relax at home, something his wife has been doing non-stop all week.

Until the wife becomes involved in some of the activities available to expatriates, she is likely to have great problems filling her time during her stay in Korea.

Children

Many children adjust to life abroad faster than their parents, but expatriate children in Korea have their own special problems. These vary a lot depending on the age and character of the child.

Young children will be touched, patted and pinched, sometimes in places Westerners consider private. Black and blond children especially will draw attention wherever they go. Preschool children may at first feel left out, not knowing the language, but before long they will speak Korean better than anyone in the family.

Older children may also be self-conscious about being stared at. They have the usual difficulty of making friends that all children experience when they move. As most expatriates in Korea stay for a limited period, their friends are constantly moving away. Some children may miss the different activities they left behind in their home communities.

Single People

People coming to Korea with a spouse and/or children are cushioned against some of the frustrations of culture shock. They can at least talk about their difficulties with someone who understands and cares. Single people have no such support system.

Singles do, however, have good opportunities to get to know Koreans and other expatriates. Koreans are very sympathetic towards people who are alone, and they are particularly eager to act as a guide, and to spend time with a foreigner. Other single expatriates are also quite supportive of those in a similar situation.

For single men, and to a certain extent for single women, there are many chances in Korea for interaction with the opposite sex. There are women eager to learn about foreign men, some even inclined towards a serious relationship with one. Likewise, many Korean men are quite eager to meet foreign women.

Relationships between Koreans and expatriates of different sexes can be the cause of many misunderstandings. Few Koreans view such encounters casually, and many presume that certain behaviour or a relationship that lasts implies a long-term, serious commitment.

Some single expatriate women in Korea have found difficulty making close friends. There are many fewer expatriate women in Korea with whom to associate. While expatriate men can easily drink with Korean men, Korean women are not as accessible for friendship with expatriate women, and Korean men are not accustomed to platonic relationships with women.

Another situation that most single expatriates run into often is related to their being unattached. Many Koreans assume that if a person is at or over the marriageable age, he or she is eager to marry. They cannot comprehend how a 28-year-old woman could be satisfied in an unmarried state. It is quite possible that single expatriates of both sexes will be introduced to potential marriage partners by well-meaning colleagues and friends. For some, this will be fun; for others, rather uncomfortable.

Missionaries

Most missionaries come to Korea expecting to stay for an extended period of time, at least six to ten years. In this respect they are unlike businessmen who can take comfort from the fact that the irritations of a different culture need be tolerated for a brief stay. Consequently, for missionaries, adjusting to Korea assumes greater importance.

A frustration of many missionaries is not being able to get down to work for a long period. Most of them spend two years in language study before they can do much missionary work, and the long wait offers few rewards, besides making them feel somewhat useless. It can be an especially difficult period when one does not appear to be progressing satisfactorily with language lessons.

Missionaries in Korea do have some advantages over other expatriates. One is the strong support from missionaries already in Korea. There is a close, family-like feeling for most from the day they arrive and this help from experienced, interested expatriates cannot be overestimated.

Then there is the esteemed place missionaries hold in the eyes of most Koreans. The dedication, generosity and sincerity of missionaries are highly admired, even by non-Christian Koreans. This, combined with the language ability they acquire, makes many of their interactions with Koreans positive. Naturally, this is true when interacting with other Christians, but it is also true when relating to people at the market, on the bus, or at a tourist site.

Non-Korean Spouses of Koreans

A number of interracial marriages exist between Koreans and Westerners, the majority between Korean women and Western men, though the reverse also happens. The couples and their families are in the unique position of having one foot in the door of Korean society, and the other foot out.

The logistics of living in Korea can be managed more successfully when one person in the family is fluent in the language and knowledgeable about the culture. There will also probably be the support of friends and family of the Korean spouse, who can ease the transition into Korea. There is usually, in addition, a vested interest in living in Korea and learning about Korean culture.

It sometimes happens, though, that these couples have trouble understanding and accepting each other's culture shock. Koreans who have lived abroad for any length of time will experience a different kind of adjustment problem that an insensitive non-Korean spouse may brush off as not important. The Korean spouse may misinterpret some of the non-Korean's unhappiness in the country as criticism of Korea, and essentially of that partner's roots. Children in such families may be confused about their identities. Families in this situation need to pay special attention to the experiences of other family members.

In these interracial marriages, there is also potential for family-in-law difficulties. Korean families are very close, and generally want to be intimately involved in one another's lives. The non-Korean spouse needs to be aware of traditional Korean family behaviour. At the same time, the Korean spouse needs to remember that such close involvement is not the norm for people coming from Western cultures.

Still another difficulty is the stigma attached to interracial marriages. Though this prejudice is diminishing with time, many Koreans still look down on people who marry out of their own culture. This is particularly true when the woman is Korean and the man Western. Strangers on the street may make derogatory comments about such couples, which are quite unpleasant to hear.

Americans

The United States is viewed positively by most Koreans. They truly appreciate the US help given during the Korean War, and her continued military and economic support. American expatriates are both envied and appreciated.

But there is a growing vocal minority openly critical of the United States. During student demonstrations, the US often comes in for criticism. Some Korean businessmen are critical of US trade policies. Consequently, perhaps more than any other nationality in Korea, American expatriates will find themselves representing and defending their country.

Non-American Westerners

Many Koreans assume that anyone who is not Asian is American. British, French and Australians get tired of hearing 'Meegook Sahram' (American) from children on the street.

It is frustrating to always be identified as someone you are not. The reason for this confusion is that by far the majority of expatriates in Korea are American. And most of the foreign movies shown in Korea are for Americans. In fact, the Korean term for 'American' has all but replaced the term for 'foreigner'.

Non-Koreans of Korean Ancestry

People of Korean ancestry who were born or lived much of their lives outside Korea have special problems which add to culture shock. Many of them came to Korea to learn about their roots. Adopted children want to learn the language, or see the country of their birth. Second and third generation Koreans from other countries have perhaps grown up eating some Korean foods, and learning some Korean customs, and they may have come here to meet their relatives. Such Koreans have a special interest in Korea, and a particular eagerness to understand and accept Korean culture.

It is this group that is the least accepted by Korean society. When a Western-looking expatriate speaks elementary Korean in a taxi, for example, the driver is especially pleased that he has made an effort to learn the language. But when a person of Korean ancestry speaks a little hesitant Korean, the driver is liable to blame his parents for not teaching their child Korean, even when the person's adoptive parents are non-Korean.

The same is true of dress style and behaviour. Whereas other Westerners can be excused for dressing and behaving in a manner different from Koreans, no such excuses would be offered on behalf of people of Korean blood.

Negative reactions in Korea are especially hurtful as these same people are identified as Korean in their home country, and may have believed that in South Korea they could finally belong. Once in Korea, they realise that culturally they are not Korean at all.

It is also more difficult for people of Korean ancestry to deal with negative aspects of living in Korea. As they are often identified as Korean, they want it to be a country they can be proud of. They have a stake in liking this country.

The restrictions of Korean society apply to people of Korean descent, but so do some of the benefits. Non-Koreans, however long they live in the country, will never be totally accepted in Korean society. People of Korean ancestry, on the other hand, even though they think and act like their Western-looking counterparts, can sometimes be accepted in Korea. They are included in the group '*uri nara sahram*' or 'our country's people'. It may be hard for such expatriates to establish close relationships, but once they do, there can be a closer bond. This special closeness applies only to people who share the Korean cultural and biological heritage.

Japanese

As a result of the early Japanese invasions of the southern coast, and their more recent annexation of Korea, the people here do not hold Japan or the Japanese in high esteem. Japanese expatriates living in Korea have many hurdles to overcome.

Other Asians

Asians have the distinct advantage of being able to blend in with Koreans. Koreans do not stare at Asians, nor will they go up to them to practise conversation. These are two of the more difficult things for non-Asians to deal with while living in Korea.

The advantage can turn into a disadvantage as soon as an Asian starts to speak. Koreans expect Asians to speak Korean. They may sometimes even think such people are only pretending not to understand Korean for their own advantage. Some insist on speaking Korean with other Asians.

There are Asian expatriates who also feel that they are considered less important than non-Asian expatriates.

MANAGING CULTURE SHOCK

Recognising that culture shock is a normal reaction to an abnormal situation, which arises out of your own expectation that people are all the same, is helpful in diminishing the sting of culture shock. Important, too, is acknowledging your feelings of frustration, instead of letting them prevent you from making observations about the situation. There are other things that you may do as well.

Read About Korea Before You Arrive

If you have time, it is much better to come to Korea with some knowledge about the country that will be your new home. The more you understand about Korea, the better prepared you will be when you arrive. The information in this book is a good start in helping you understand Korean customs and culture. If you are interested in art, history, dance, antiques or Korean cuisine, some reading about those particular topics will give you something to look forward to in your new country.

Meet Other Expatriates

Many close friendships have been made while shopping for tennis shoes or silk ties in Itaewon, just because two people are expatriates: they have something important in common.

It seems that once in a foreign country, an expatriate can feel quite comfortable with almost any other foreigner, even those quite unlike friends back home. In Korea, most differences in education, age, economic level or even personality seem minor compared to the similarities of being expatriates.

If you are new, longer-staying expatriates can identify with your difficulties easily. All of them have stories of the problems they had when they first came to Korea, and they are eager to share their store of knowledge as well as suggestions to make your adjustment easier. Experienced expatriates can save newcomers untold hassles.

Some expatriates tell of not seeing a single foreigner for their first six months in Korea. That may be an overstatement, unless one resides in a small village in the country, but it is true that some foreigners do not know how to make contact with other expatriates. It is not very difficult.

If the children go to a foreign school, it is easy to meet other parents at the school. FOCUS (see page 238) has regular meetings and a hotline to call for general and specific information. There are business organisations for expatriate business people, and many organisations for women. Within these larger organisations are many special interest groups. There are several churches in languages other than Korean, and some of the Korean adoption agencies have volunteer activities for expatriate women. The list is endless.

When meeting other expatriates, it is natural to complain about things which may not be available or reminisce about life back home. Be wary of friends who isolate themselves in the cocoon of the expatriate community and use these friendships to support their withdrawal from Korea. Frustrations need to be validated but too much criticism of the host culture can facilitate negative expectations and prevent one from understanding the deeper cultural meanings behind stressful interactions.

Re-create Your Own World

While it will certainly be impossible to make living arrangements identical to what you had back home, do make an effort to personalise your living space. Put up pictures, use familiar bedspreads, and make sure you have got your favourite frying pan. When so much of your environment is foreign, any familiar article gives comfort.

Make a noticeboard with updated pictures of friends and family. Take advantage of the inexpensive flowers, and make up a bouquet of your favourite variety. If you have children, be sure to bring their own

Fortunately, there are some familiar Western chain stores and fast food outlets that help alleviate culture shock.

stuffed animals to make their rooms feel familiar. Bring tapes of your favourite music, to listen to when you want to hear the sounds of home. And do not forget your favourite books.

These small steps may seem insignificant, but they really do make your somewhat different-looking home a place to feel at ease. With all the exotic and unusual things that confront you outside, you need a haven of comfort for a retreat.

But as one begins to understand Korea better, Korean objects will almost unconsciously become part of your home, soon to be treasured possessions just as your experience in Korea becomes a part of who you are.

Meet Koreans of a Similar Social Level

One of the best ways to understand Korea, and to begin the process of enjoying the culture, is through Korean friends. These friends can explain what you do not understand about the country, show you around, and counteract any negative encounters you have had with other Koreans. Your maid, the fruit-seller and the shopkeeper in Itaewon are not the right people. Since Koreans rarely have friendships with people who are not their social equals, you will probably be most satisfied with Korean friends with a background similar to yours. Meeting such friends requires a special effort on your part.

They can most easily be found at some of the same places you meet expatriate friends: international schools, churches and social organisations. Koreans who have lived abroad and wish to keep contact with foreigners are likely to appear there. They are also probably eager to help you get along in Korea, especially having experienced the difficulties of living in a foreign culture themselves.

Learn the Korean Language

This is a rather obvious suggestion, but do not overlook it. Korean is a difficult language for most non-Koreans to learn. Even people who study full-time for a year cannot speak the language fluently. Since many Koreans at tourist attractions and at stores catering to foreigners can communicate sufficiently in English, you may think you can get along well without any language ability. It is still worthwhile, however, to spend as much time as you can studying the language. When Koreans hear you use even a little Korean, they feel that you value their country and language.

If you learn some basic Korean, for example the numbers and a few questions about prices and bargaining, you can survive well in the market. To get a Korean to understand you in a language so different from your own will give you a sense of satisfaction. You will not feel so alienated when some Korean words start to sound familiar, even if you cannot understand exactly what is said.

There is a variety of Korean classes available. Some are quite intense, almost full-time. Others are less demanding, but are ideal for those with less time to invest in language learning. These programmes are advertised in the English-language newspapers.

Language classes are also a good place to meet other newcomers. No matter what the age, nationality or economic level, the students usually feel a special kinship in their common endeavour to master an exotic language.

One encouraging note about learning Korean is that reading it is very easy. Some people can learn the phonetic alphabet in a few hours. The slowest person can learn it in a week. Once you can sound out the signs on the street, even though you do not know the meaning, you will feel as though you are in a more familiar setting. You may enjoy sounding out some of the many English words that are written in *hangul,* the Korean alphabet.

Do Not Expect Too Much of Yourself

Adjusting to a new climate, new food, a new home and new friends, to say nothing of the new culture, is not easy. Newcomers cannot expect to arrive one day and be settled in a week later. Opening a new bank account will not be as simple as it was back home. You cannot expect to order things for your home as painlessly as you did in your own country. Some things you want or need may not exist here. Others take much longer to locate or to be made. Koreans do not understand your strange taste, and they may be surprised when you will not accept a sofa that is 'almost' like the one you ordered (bright red instead of tan).

Jet lag can take more than a week to overcome. The new diet can be difficult to assimilate. Most newcomers find that just living in a new culture tires them, as so many new stimuli bombard the senses. Your body needs time to settle in. Do not expect it to go full steam. Even long-term expatriates find that they seem never to regain the energy they had in their own country. Being regarded as strange by everyone else, trying to understand Korean thinking and behaviour, and worrying that you are always doing something wrong may make you chronically tired.

It is important to recognise that culture shock will take its physical toll on you. Do not blame yourself when you are not as efficient or energetic as you were back home.

Lower Your Expectations of Others

Just as you yourself will not perform at peak level, your spouse and children will also have difficulties settling in. Culture shock affects everyone. They may do things that were not acceptable back home. Try to understand them and relax some of your expectations. If your children want to stay up and talk past their normal bedtime, do not let it bother you. If your spouse is not quite as tidy as he or she used to be, hold your breath. After an initial adjustment period, many things will return to normal.

The same applies to Koreans who provide services for you. Though you may be quite specific in your instructions, you will often find that things do not get done exactly as you had requested. Your secretary may not understand that when you said 'urgent', you meant 'now'. The people who custom-made your bed might have thought 'king size' and 'double' were the same. Try to relax and be patient. The language and cultural gap between you and them is at its biggest at first. It may take you a while to learn how to make yourself understood.

Consciously Pursue Special Interests

There are hundreds of interests to explore in Korea. By focusing on those things you like and can do, your dissatisfaction with the things you cannot do in Korea will be minimised. All kinds of art classes are available, from calligraphy to water colours to ceramics. Some are not taught in English, but in such classes, language fluency is not always necessary.

Shopping for antiques can be a new interest for expatriates. The main area for antiques in Seoul is Insadong, although there are a growing number of stores in Itaewon.

Any interest in sightseeing or photography can be pursued in depth. You will have opportunities to see things you have never seen in your home country.

Sports fans of all kinds have settled quite happily into Korean life. Tennis, golf, volleyball, soccer, hiking, martial arts, swimming, scuba diving, skiing, boating and camping can all be enjoyed in Korea. Some expatriates find they can devote more time to such sports in Korea than they could in their native country.

People interested in the performing arts will never be bored. World-renowned orchestras, ballet companies and drama groups make their way to Seoul every year. And Korea has her own unique and fascinating dance groups and play companies. Most of these are listed in the English language newspapers.

Connoisseurs of ethnic food will have many opportunities to develop their interests as well. Of course Korean foods of all kinds are widely available, as well as Japanese and Chinese foods. Hotels often import chefs from Western countries to prepare a special menu for a week or month. All kinds of superb foods are offered at different times throughout the year. Seoul International Women's Association (see page 238) offers a variety of classes in ethnic cooking.

By becoming involved in activities, an expatriate can begin to appreciate living in Korea. It is easier for those in Seoul to find activities of interest, but expatriates living in outlying areas are rarely far from a major city, where they, too, can find something to enrich their lives.

Remember: Life Back Home Was Not Trouble-free

After a few weeks, months or years, there is a tendency for many expatriates to think only about the good things in their home country. They remember how cheap and delicious bananas used to be, how nice it was to walk unnoticed on the street, and how spacious the roads were. The negative aspects of life back home are often neglected. In this light, home seems to be the perfect culture. Natural longings for the familiar will become dreams of a non-existent country.

True, you can understand situations better in your own country. But certainly things were not perfect. Every job, house and community has faults, and some of those faults are not found in Korea.

After returning to their home countries, some expatriates have found themselves missing many things about living in Korea. Doubtless, you will, too. The Korean environment is more family oriented. Businessmen are usually more highly regarded in Korea than they would be in their home countries. Housewives have more free time to pursue their own interests, with maids to take care of the housework. Many families here have nicer housing, provided by their employer, than they could afford back home.

When you begin to dream about life in your home country, remember that before long you must face the reality there. And then you will be dreaming about life in Korea.

Recognise That Culture Shock Relapses Often Occur

After you have organised your office and home, become a part of various organisations, found ways to pursue meaningful activities, learned how to get around Seoul satisfactorily, and even come to appreciate many of the unique elements in Korean society as well as in individual Korean friends, there will still be times when all that learning seems for naught, when nothing makes sense any more and when all you can think about is being back where people do things the 'right' way. Will this mean that what you had thought was cultural adjustment was really just a short-term adaptation? Thankfully, the answer to that question is often no.

There will be times when an unfulfilled expectation will catch you off guard and your reaction to it will again be one of anxiety or aversion. Even long-term residents of Korea continue to encounter new situations daily, many of them puzzling and the source of confusion and irritation. Perhaps your secretary will laugh after losing the text for a forthcoming speech, or someone pushes their way in front of you just as you reach the head of the supermarket line. Such an incident may trigger a number of uncomplimentary thoughts about your host country, usually thoughts beginning with 'Why do they...?'

Your frustration is natural and predictable. And you'll need to address it in the same way you dealt with it earlier in your adjustment, by realising the source of your stress is coming from your assumption that everyone thinks, feels and behaves as you do. Instead of condemning the incident which makes you feel apprehensive and bothered, among other things, observe the situation and label the cause of those feelings. Express your frustration to a confidant without assigning blame to the secretary or energetic customer, for it is your expectations, not their actions, which are responsible for your misery. And remember that it is just such experiences that are giving you a new understanding of yourself, your own culture and even Korea, a country so different from your own, but one in which you will learn not only to survive, but to thrive.

CULTURAL QUIZ

Reading about Korean culture is one thing. Actually living in Korea is another. The purpose of this quiz is to help you imagine some of the situations that might confront you while you are living in Korea.

Ten of the most common difficulties that newcomers to Korea come across are described below. There are several alternative answers to choose from. A discussion follows about why some answers are better than others.

SITUATION 1

A Korean neighbour stops by your house to deliver your mail, which had inadvertently been left at her home. You begin a friendly

conversation, during which you offer her some coffee. She politely refuses. What should you do?

A   Take her answer at face value, and drop the subject.

B   Bring her coffee anyway.

C   A little later, ask her if she wants coffee again.

D   Assume that she's Buddhist, and offer her tea as Buddhists don't drink coffee.

Comments

In Korea it is sometimes considered rude to accept something right away. So her refusal may well be out of politeness. When someone visits your home, it is always proper to serve your guest something, and serving something is probably more important than if the guest actually enjoys what you serve.

The best answer in this case would be *C*, but if she refuses again, bring her refreshment anyhow. Answer *B* would be second best. In fact, it is acceptable to bring something to your guest without consulting her first. Sometimes sugar and cream are added to coffee without consulting the guest.

Answer *A* would be considered rude, and answer *D* is simply not true.

SITUATION 2

You are out drinking with some Korean colleagues. Shortly after you arrive, the waitress brings glasses and a few bottles of beer. One colleague hands a glass to you. What do you do?

A   Pass the glass on to the person next to you.

B   Hold it while your colleague fills it, then hand him an empty glass to hold while you pour.

C   Fill it and hand it back to the person who gave it to you.

D   Consider it an honour, and fill it and all the other glasses with beer, one for each person present.

Comments

In social drinking, it is normal for a person to hand an empty glass to another person. The receiver should hold the glass as the giver pours the alcohol, as in answer B. Later, the receiver should pour alcohol for his drinking partner.

Answers A, C and D will all be met with confused and embarrassed smiles.

SITUATION 3

You get on a crowded city bus. There is no place to sit, so you stand next to a seated woman. A few minutes later you feel the woman pulling at your package. What do you do?

A   Hand her your package, since it is not worth much, and assume she is collecting for a charity.

B   Scream in any language you know, to prevent her from stealing your money.

C   Give her your package and smile.

Comments

It is common etiquette in Korea for seated passengers on buses to hold the packages of those standing. This is usually done nonverbally. Answer *C* is the best answer.

Answer *A* would be all right, but you would be surprised when she gave it back to you as she got off the bus. Answer *B* would embarrass the woman as well as yourself.

SITUATION 4

You are at a party and start up a friendly conversation with a person you have met only a few times. One of the first questions he asks you is 'Why aren't you married?' You do not wish to answer. What do you do?

A   Explain that it is none of his business, and walk away as soon as possible.

B   Joke that there are no partners good enough for you.

C   Lie that you are married already.

D   Ignore the question and change the subject.

Comments

Personal questions are seen as a way to show one's concern for another. In no way does the person mean to be nosy. Answer *D* would be the best answer.

Answer *A* would damage the other person's *kibun*. If the lie in answer *C* were found out, you would not be viewed favourably. Answer *B* may be viewed as a joke, but it may be seen as a lack of humbleness.

SITUATION 5

On your birthday, a former Korean student drops by your house with a small gift. What do you do?

A Invite him in, thank him for the gift, and offer him something to drink.

B Invite him in, open the gift in his presence, and ask him to stay for the next meal.

C Tell him you appreciate the thought, but that you cannot accept such a gift. This is done to prevent the obligation of any favours.

D   Thank him for the gift and remember to find out his birthday so that you can send him a gift on that day.

Comments

Koreans consider the relationship between teacher and student to be lifelong. It is not unusual for a student to give his teacher a gift, even when the teacher is no longer teaching him.

Answer *A* is the best answer. Answer *B* is impolite because after the gift is opened the giver might be embarrassed at how small it is. Returning the gift, as in answer *C*, would be rude and unnecessary. Teachers have no obligations to a student because of a small gift. Nor is it appropriate for a teacher to give a birthday gift to a student, as in answer *D*. The teacher is obviously of higher status.

SITUATION 6

You are walking down the street with friend Mr A. He meets Mr B, whom you do not know. After a few minutes, you realise that you are

227

being excluded from the conversation, and that you have not even been introduced. What do you do?

A   Do not worry about it. Assume that Mr B is someone you do not need to know.

B   Do not say anything, thinking that Mr A is indirectly insulting you.

C   Introduce yourself to Mr B.

D   Quietly mention to Mr A that you have not been introduced to Mr B.

Comments

It is not usual for people who meet casually to introduce their companions. A chance meeting will probably last only a few minutes, after which each person will go his own way. Answer A is best.

Answer B is totally incorrect. Answers C and D would make everyone uncomfortable. Remember that if there is any reason for you to meet the other person, your friend would introduce you.

SITUATION 7

You are driving your car along a city street on a beautiful, seemingly peaceful afternoon. Suddenly, you hear a loud siren blaring on and off. Other cars pull over, and a man motions for you to do the same. What do you do?

A   Ignore the man and quickly make your way to your country's embassy.

B   Pull your car over to the side of the road. Lie down on the floor of your car.

C   Pull your car over and sneak into a nearby coffee shop for 20 minutes.

Comments

If you remember the date, this is probably happening on or around the 15th of the month. It is the monthly civil defence drill. The siren can scare the newly arrived expatriate. People must get off the road, but

remaining in one's car is acceptable. It is best to take shelter in a nearby building, making *C* the best answer.

If you proceeded to head towards your embassy, as in answer *A*, you would meet strong resistance. Lying down, as in answer *B*, is unnecessary.

SITUATION 8

It is the middle of January and you are trying to figure out some way of lowering your enormous heating bill without dying of pneumonia. Your maid comes to work and the first thing she does is to open all the windows and begin cleaning. What do you do?

A Assume she thinks your apartment is too hot, and question her sanity.

B Realise that she is indirectly asking to be fired, and kindly let her go.

C Explain to her that you never want the windows open in the winter.

Comments

Koreans tend to like their homes warmer than their Western counter-parts. But they feel that fresh air, every day, is very important. They also believe that when one is cleaning, the windows must be open so that the dust can get out. (Apparently, Korean dust never *enters* through the window!)

Most homes in Korea are heated by the *ondol* system of hot water pipes beneath the floor. Traditionally, the walls of the home did not keep heat in very well, so the best way to keep warm was to sit on the warm floor. Sitting there, open doors or windows were not a problem.

Answer *C* is the only appropriate answer, but you may need to make an effort to enforce such a policy. In the summer, wire mesh anti-insect screens are thought to keep in the dust while cleaning. So, before cleaning, your maid will probably open all the screens.

SITUATION 9

You have heard about an end-of-year office party for a few days, but have received no formal invitation. One day, a colleague informs you that the boss will be hosting the party at his house. What do you do?

A   Ask your colleague when the party begins, and go.
B   Assume that since you were not invited by the boss, you had better not go. Naturally, you feel hurt.
C   Assume that the boss has your best interests at heart, and did not invite you because you would feel uncomfortable at the party.
D   Casually ask the boss if he knows anything about the party.

Comments

Invitations in Korea are almost always informal, and often not made by the person hosting the event. Other people in your office probably know when the party is, and your colleague made a special point of telling you, since you may not have understood the Korean chatter about the party. Answer *A* is clearly best.

Since you are part of the office, any party given for the office would include you. Your being foreign is irrelevant. Answers *B* and *C* are incorrect for that reason.

There is nothing wrong with asking the boss, as in answer *D*, but it is really unnecessary. And he may worry that he had inadvertently hurt your feelings by not clearly inviting you.

SITUATION 10

You are enjoying a drink after a lovely dinner with a group of your closest Korean friends, who are of the same sex as yourself. Much to your dismay, you realise that the hand of one friend is resting on your thigh. What do you do?

A   After realising that this 'friendship' has a different meaning for your friend, you make an excuse and escape quickly.

B   Realising that this is one way of showing friendship in Korea, you reciprocate by resting your hand on your friend's thigh.

C   Feeling uncomfortable, you quietly say that in your home country, people do not do this.

D   Accept his touch without reciprocating.

Comments

In Korea, physical expression between people of the same sex is natural and comfortable. There is no homosexual connotation to such behaviour. Answer *A* would be totally incorrect. If you feel comfortable, answer *B* would be a good answer, or answer *D*. If not, it is best to let your friend know, as in answer *C*

DO'S AND DON'TS APPENDIX

GENERAL

Do

- Show affection as a sign of friendship between people of the same sex.

- Remember that Koreans express their affection for children through touching them. Once used to it, children enjoy the attention given to them.

- Remember you are expected to bargain in markets. After asking the price, give the seller a counter-offer. Finally, agree on a price somewhere between the seller's offer and your own. Bargaining is not done at supermarkets, department stores, or other places where the price of merchandise is already marked.

- Bow when greeting another person for the first time in a day. If the discrepancy in status is very great, only the person of lower status bows, while the other responds verbally. When two people are introduced, they also bow.

- Treat the elderly with kindness and respect at all times. Bus seats should always be offered to them. If an elderly person has trouble crossing the street, or trouble carrying something, a younger person is obliged to help.

- Preserve social harmony at all costs; you may have to tell small lies, or adopt indirect, less efficient behaviour than in the West.

- Remember that status is very important. It is determined primarily by profession, family and age. Acknowledging other people's status will make social relationships smoother. It is also necessary to act according to one's own status. For example, a maid's status is lower than that of their employer and they are most comfortable working when that distinction is clear.

- Do address Koreans, by their title, for example, Manager Kim, President Lee, Assistant Director Park. This shows respect and helps to identify the innumerable Mr Kims, Mr Lees and Miss Parks. If you can learn to say the titles in Korean, a closer feeling will be established.

- Pass objects to someone of equal or higher status with the right hand. To show the most respect, two hands are used, or the right hand supported by the left. When passing objects to people of lower status, either hand is acceptable, but using two hands is not appropriate.

- Remember that highly educated people are respected, and what they say is listened to carefully.

- Remove all footwear before entering someone's home, or when entering a temple. In offices and other public places, shoes are not removed.

- Remember that the same public bathrooms are sometimes used by both men and women. Women walk past men's urinals on their way to private booths. Bathrooms in homes often have wet floors, so plastic thongs are worn whenever entering the bathroom.

Don't

- Show affection between the sexes in public.

- Show your anger. It is impolite, and can permanently damage interpersonal relationships. Keep your temper at all times.

- Criticize. When absolutely necessary, it must be done tact fully, gently and privately.

- Dress too informally. The way you dress reflects your position. Also, it is a sign of respect, so when meeting people, or when visiting someone's home, one should dress nicely and conservatively. Shorts, backless dresses, and so on are not appropriate in public.

- Expose money unless you are paying at the market or at a store. When giving a gift of money or when paying an employee, money should be put in an envelope.

- Be impatient when services are not performed on time, some one is late, or things are not done efficiently.

- Answer personal questions if you do not wish to answer them. Simply change the subject. These questions may include 'Why aren't you married?' and 'How old are you?' and are simply a way Koreans use to get to know another person.

BUSINESS

Do

- Always get a third party formally to introduce you to a potential business associate. Self-introductions are rarely successful in Korea.

- Always carry business cards, preferably printed in English and Korean, and make sure that you give one to business acquaintances during the introduction.

- Establish a good relationship before you discuss any business. Develop social networks, both among expatriates and Koreans, to help you in future business transactions.

- Remember that in Korean society, smooth social relationships often take precedence over business efficiency.

- Recognise that entertaining is an essential part of doing business, and that the cost of entertaining may far exceed what it costs in your home country.

- Be flexible at all times. Pushing too hard will not be viewed favourably.

- Remember that 'yes' does not always mean 'yes'.

Don't

- Assume that everyone in Korea understands your language. Get into the habit of having people paraphrase what you say, and do not be afraid to write down key points.

- Cause anyone to lose face. Always allow an 'escape'.

- Use the telephone for business communication. Use face to face contact.

- Criticise anything Korean.

DINING AND ENTERTAINMENT

Do

- Remember that invitations are generally given informally. They are usually verbal, and not always given by the person hosting the event. Invitations are rarely given more than a few days in advance, and sometimes only a few hours before the event.

- Prepare gifts. Fruit, flowers, cakes or alcohol should be given whenever visiting someone's home. On special occasions, such as a first birthday, a gift is also appropriate. When one attends a wedding, a 60th birthday party or a funeral, money in an envelope is appropriate.

- Prepare more food for guests than would be necessary by Western standards. Generosity towards friends and acquaintances is important. This includes giving gifts that are worth a bit more than one might expect. Being at all stingy is impolite.

- Remember that drinking is an important part of social and business relationships for men in Korea. The amount of alcohol consumed at any given time is generally considerably more than most Westerners are accustomed to consuming.

- Be prepared to sing a song or two at any social gathering. At parties, the most honoured person is given the first chance to sing. Other people are then each given a turn.

- Remember that eating is done with chopsticks and a large spoon. Rice is served on the left, and soup on the right. The person of highest status should begin the meal. Excessive talking during the meal is considered impolite. Slurping is acceptable, as a sign of enjoyment.

- Remember to eat your kimchee cautiously at first as it is usually quite spicy. Kimchee is the national food made from pickled Chinese or napa cabbage. Koreans will be very pleased to see you enjoy your kimchee.

- Remember that paying is considered an honour and also a matter of pride. Paying is done by the person who did the inviting. 'Going Dutch' is never done. If there is a question as to who made the invitation, the bill is fought over.

Don't

- Waste rice. Rice is the staple of the Korean diet. Throwing away leftover rice is considered wasteful and bad luck.

- Tip before checking if a service charge has already been added to the bill. This is done in some first-class hotels. However, if the service at a restaurant, hairdresser or in a taxi has been especially good, a small tip would be appreciated.

GLOSSARY

USEFUL WORDS AND PHRASES

Greetings and Common Courtesy

How do you do?

Good morning/afternoon/evening
or How are you?
Thank you.
I am sorry.
I am glad to see/meet you.
Come in.
Good bye.
Yes, there is/we have.

Cho-um peop-gessoyo?
(informal)
Annyong haseyo.
(used any time of day)
kamsa-hamnida.
Mee-an hamnida.
Mannaso pan-gawoyo.
Tul-o oseyo.
Annyong he gaseyo.
Ye, issoyo.

Transportation

Will you show/tell me the way
   to the Seoul City Hall?
Where is the ballpoint pen?
Where can I get a taxi?
Over there.
How long does it take to Seoul
railroad station?
It takes about 15 minutes.
Please stop here/over there.
How far is it to
Kwanghwamoon?
Does this bus go to Kangnam?

*Seoul shi-chong kanun kilul
karucho chuseyo?*
Ballpoint pen e odi issumnika?
Odeso taxi-rul talsoo itsul kayo?
Cho-ke yo.
*Seoul-yeok kkaji olmana kollim-
ni ka?*
Yak ship-o-boon kollimnida.
Yogi/chogi so sewo chuseyo.
*Kwanghwamoon ggaji olmana
momneka?*
Yee bus-ka Kangnam kamneka?

Shopping

Please show me this wristwatch.	*E-shegye rul poyo chooseyo.*
How much is it?	*E-geot-eun olma imnika?*
I would like to buy this.	*E-geot-ul sa-ke-sumnida.*
Please wait for a moment.	*Chom-shi keedalyo cheseyo.*

Eating out

May I have a menu, please?	*Menu chom chuseyo.*
What is your specialty here?	*Chal-hanun umsik-e mu-eot ip-nika?*
What would you recommend?	*Muosi mashi-isumnika?*
Give me the same as his/hers.	*Katun kosuro cheseyo.*
Don't make it too spicy.	*Nomu maep-chi-anke hae-chuseyo.*
Give me one-portion (two-, three-).	*Il-in-boon (e-in-boon, sam-in-boon) chuseyo.*
It is delicious.	*Mashi-soyo.*
Please give me a glass of water.	*Mool chooseyo.*
Please give me some more of this.	*E-geot teo chuseyo.*
I enjoyed the meal.	*Chal mogosumnida.*
Check, please.	*Kyesanso chuseyo.*
How much is it?	*Olma imnika?*
It is W5,000/10,000/15,000/20,000/30,000.	*O-chon/maan/maan o-chon/e-maan/saam man won imnida.*
Can I pay it with my credit card?	*Kredit kaduro kyesan halsu isumnika?*

Accommodation

Do you have any vacancy?	*Bin-bang isumnika?*
No, we don't.	*Aniyo, op-sumnida.*
What hotel can I call for a room?	*O-nu hotel-ae chon-hwa halkayo?*

Frequently Used Words

bank	*eunhaeng*
hospital	*pyong-won*
police station	*kyochalso*
post office	*woo-chae-gook*
school	*hakkyo*
toilet	*hwajangshil*
address	*chooso*
automobile	*jadongcha*
bicycle	*jajungo*
book	*chaek*
breakfast	*achim shiksa*
currency/check	*hyngeum/soo-pyo*
dinner	*joyok-shiksa*
funeral	*changrye shik*
house	*jib*
lunch	*jomshim*
men's/women's clothing	*namja/yeoja ot*
money	*ton*
name	*erum, songmyong*
shoes	*shin, kootoo*
sleeping	*jam*
socks	*yangmal*
stamp	*woo-pyo*
wedding	*kyol hon*
spring/summer/autumn/winter	*pom/yeorum/ka-eul/kyo-eul*
hot/cold/warm (temperature)	*ttu-keo-un/cha-ga-un/ttatteut-han*
east/west/south/north	*tong/seo/nam/book*
hot/salty/sweet/bitter	*maep-ssumnida/tchamnida/ shinggop-sumnida/ssumnida*

brother/sister	*hyongje/nooe*
father/mother	*aboji/omoni*
grandfather/grandmother	*haraboji/halmoni*
grandparents	*chobumo*
grandson/granddaughter	*sonja/sonnyo*
policeman/policewoman	*kyongchal*
professor/teacher	*kyo-shoo/sunsaeng*

Commonly Used English Words

Virtually everyone uses and/or understands these words:

ballpoint pen
baseball
bell
bicycle
bowling
car
coffee/coffee shop
college
cooking
dancing
golf
goodbye
ink
milk
money
sex
soccer
tea
tea room
tennis
university

RESOURCE GUIDE

GENERAL

Customs Tel 653-3041 (Seoul); 665-3100 (Kimpo). **Immigration** Tel 653-3041 (Seoul); 664-7611 (Kimpo). **Foreign Workers' Human Rights** Tel 795-5504. **Volunteer Lawyers** Tel 522-5504.

FOCUS (Foreigners Community Service) Tel 798-7529/797-8212. The group assists expatriates living in Korea, and provides up-to-date information on everything from finding housing to what kinds of food are available in Korea. FOCUS has a team of medical personnel available for emergency referrals 24 hours a day (Tel 798-7529/797-8212) and also provides dental referrals. Website: **http://www.focusonseoul.com**

TOURIST INFORMATION, TRANSPORTATION, AND CURRENCY

Tourist Information

Korea Tourist Information Center: (02) 757-0086
Gimpo, or Kimpo, International Airport Information Center: Terminal 1; (02) 665-0088, and Terminal 2; (02) 665-0986
Seoul City Tourist Information Center: (02) 731-6337
Gimhae International Airport Information Center: (051) 973-1100
Jeju International Airport Information Center: (064) 742-0032
Jeju Jungmun Tourist Information Center: (064) 738-8550

Korean National Tourism Association Main Office (KNTO): 10 Da-dong, Jung-gu, Seoul 100-180, Korea. Tel: 82-2-7299-600, fax: 82-2-757-5997. Website: **http://www.knto.or.kr/**

Overseas Offices
U. S. A. & Canada:
Toll free: 800-868-7567 (North America)
Los Angeles: Tel 323-634-0280, Fax 323-634-0281, email kntola@mail.wcis.com.
New York: Tel 201-585-0909, Fax 201-585-9041, email kntony@ring3.net.
Chicago: Tel 312-981-1717/9, Fax 312-981-1721, email kntocg@idt.net
Toronto: Tel 416-348-9058, Fax 416-348-9058, email Toronto@knto.ca

Asia
Hong Kong: tel. 852-2523-8065, fax 852-2845-0765, email general@knto.com.hk
Singapore: tel. 65-6533-0441/2, fax 65-6534-3427, email kntosp@pacific.net.sg
Taipei: tel. 886-2-2720-8049, fax 886-2-2757-6414, email kntotp@ms5.hinet.net
Bangkok: tel. 66-2-231-3895, fax 66-2-231-3897,email kntobkk@knto-th.org
Beijing: tel. 86-10-8453-8213/4, fax 86-10-8453-8147, email bjknto@a-1.net.cn

Europe
Frankfurt: tel. 49-69-233226, fax 49-69-253519, email kntoff@euko.de
Paris: tel. 33-1-4538-7123, fax 33-1-4538-7471,email knto@club-internet.fr
London: Tel 44-20-7321-2535/7925-1717, Fax 44-20-7321-0876, email koreatb@dircon.co.uk
Moscow:Tel 7-095-230-6240, Fax 7-095-230-6246, email kntomc@hotbox.ru

Japan

Tokyo: Tel 81-3-3580-3941/3597-1717, Fax 81-3-3591-4601, email kokyo@knto.or.jp

Osaka: Tel 81-6-6266-0847, Fax 81-6-6266-0803, email Osaka@knto.or.jp

Fukuoka: Tel 81-92-471-7174, Fax 81-92-474-8015, email fukuoka@knto.or.jp

Nagoya: Tel 81-52-933-6550, Fax 81-52-933-6553, email Nagoya@knto.or.jp

Sendai: Tel 81-22-711-5991, Fax 81-22-711-5993, email sendai@knto.or.jp

Oceania

Sydney: Tel 61-2-9252-4147, Fax 61-2-9251-2104, email visitkorea@knto.org.au

Subway

There are excellent subway systems in Seoul, Busan, Daegu, and Inchon. The Seoul system is one of the largest and best in the world. The subway is the most efficient and convenient way for expatriates to get around town. Eight subway lines now serve the whole parts of Seoul and its suburbs. Each line is colour-coded.

Currency

The unit of Korean currency is the Won. Coin denominations are W10, W50, W100, and W500. Negotiable cashiers checks are used for larger amounts. Foreign currency and traveler's checks can be converted into Korean Won at banks and other authorized money exchangers at airports and in cities. USD $1.00 is equivalent to about W1,200. The ratio varies so it is wise to check with any local bank before departing for Korea.

EMERGENCY AND HEALTH
Emergency Numbers
Police 112 (the police also provide lost and found services). **Fire Department** 119 (only Korean is spoken). Foreigners who need police assistance can call the **Central Interpretation Centre** at 313-0842. The **International SOS Korea** provides a 24-hour emergency service for expatriates, and acts as a link between patients and Korean hospitals for a fee. The organisation can be contacted at 790-7561

Clinics for Expatriates
International Clinic Severance Yonsei University Hospital, Shinchon-dong, Tel 361-6540. **Seoul Foreign Clinic** Hannam-dong, Tel 796-1871. **Seoul Clinic Lab (Seoul Polyclinic)** Hannaro Building, Tel 735-4694 (Pediatrician)/732-3030 (General)

Hospitals
Severance Yonsei University Hospital, Shinchon-dong, Tel 361-6669/6863 (Emergency). **Assan Medical Center** Pungnap-don, Tel 2224-3331/6 (Emergency)/5002 (International).

Handicapped Facilities
Samyook Rehabilitation Centre Tel 0347-61-3636. **National Rehabilitation Centre (under the Ministry of Welfare)** Tel 901-1700. **Korean Association for the Physically Disabled** Tel 804-8751.

HOME AND FAMILY
Accommodation
Hotel accommodation and youth hostels: **Korea Hotel Association** Tel 703-2845, www.hotelskorea.or.kr. **Toursketch** Tel 3272-33223. **Korea National Tourist Organisation** www.knto.or.kr/english. **Korea Youth Hostel Association** Tel 725-3031.
Long-term accommodation: **P.L. Reality Consulting Company** Tel 795-5000, www.plrealty.com.english.html

Schools for Expatriate Children

Centennial Christian School Tel 905-9275. **Chinese Primary, Middle and High School** Tel 776-3893 (Primary), 334-9104 (Middle and High). **Deutsche Schule Seoul** Tel 792-0797. **Early Childhood Learning Center (Montessori School)** Tel 795-8418. **Ecole Francaise de Seoul** Tel 535-1158. **Global Christian School** Tel 797-0234. **Japanese School** Tel 574-0348. **International Christian School** Tel 792-4116 (Elementary)/761-9972 (High School). **Korea Kent Foreign School** Tel 2207-7091. **Seoul Academy** Tel 555-2475. **Seoul Foreign School** Tel 335-5101. **Seoul International School** Tel 2233-4551.

Housekeeping Services

FOCUS Tel 798-7529/797-8212. **YWCA** Tel 779-4900. **Doksan Women Work Centre** Tel 804-8751.

ENTERTAINMENT AND LEISURE
Specialty Restaurants and Cafés

American: **Bennigan's** Tel 766-9800. **Coco's** Tel 565-1020. **Gold Rush** Tel 741-1020. **TGI Fridays** Tel 776-0071.

Brazilian: **Ipanema** Tel 779-2756.

Chinese: **Tongbosong** Tel 754-8002. **Mallijangsong** Tel 541-3113. **Taepyongno Club** Tel 778-9222. **Hyang-won** Tel 335-0010. **Hokyungjeon** Tel 317-0494/929-7863. **Oyang** Tel 422-8886. **Sansu** Tel 799-8163. **Lotus Garden** Tel 565-5700.

German: **Memories** Tel 795-3544.

Indian: **Taj Mahal** Tel 749-0316. **Ashoka** Tel 792-0117.

Italian: **Il Ponte** Tel 317-3270. **La Cantian** Tel 777-2579. **La Cucina** Tel 794-6005. **La Fontana** Tel 2230-3379. **Ristorante Firenze** Tel 559-7606.

Japanese: **Songwon** Tel 755-3979. **Japan** Tel 2279-3945. **Songjon** 564-2244. **Kuksusa** 720-2701. **Hakada Udong** Tel 737-2700. **Ariake** Tel 2230-3356. **Hakone** Tel 559-7623.

Mexican: **Fiji Island** Tel 798-4656. **LaPaloma** Tel 411-3856.
Pakistani: **Moghul** Tel 796-5501.
Scandinavian: **Scandinavian Club** Tel 2265-9964.
Swiss: **Chalet Swiss** Tel 797-9664. **Marche** Tel 508-0231.
Thai: **Thai Orchid** Tel 792-8836.
Vegetarian: **Shigol Saenghwal** Tel 511-2402.
Vietnamese: **Rauje** Tel 741-0292.

Restaurants for Korean Cuisine: Recommended by Local Governments

Seoul

Goryeo Samgye Tang: 55-3 Seosomun-ku, Jung-gu, Tel 02-752-9376, kown for ginseng chicken soup.

Seomun Hoegwan: 120-22 Seosomun-dong, jung-gu, 02-756-0897, specialized in tenderloin.

Nampomyeonok: 125 Da-dong, Jung-gu, 02-777-2269, known for Bulgogi (thinly sliced, marianated unique Korean seasonsing and barbequed.)

Yonggeummok: 165-1 Da-dong, Jung-gu, 02-777-1689, known for mudfish soup.

Jeonjujip: 12-2 Bukchang-dong, Jung-gu, 02-752-9282, specialized in rice with mixed vegetables.

Gomguksijib: 12-1 Mugyo-dong, Jung-gu, 02-756-3249, known for noodle soup.

Busan

Jeongwon: 11-2 Donggwang-dong 2-ga, Jung-gu, 051-245-8444, grilled tenderloin.

Crystal Hansik Buffet: 1394-266 Jung 1-dong, Haeundae-gu, 051-743-6761, TKD.

Gogung Han Jeongsik: 1128-5 Jung 1-dong, Haeundae-gu, 051-742-3737, TKD.

Bugwang Garden: 1489-10 Jung 2-dong, Haeundae-gu, 051-743-0041, Galbi.

Cheong Giwa Sikdang: 655-13 U-dong, Haeundae-gu, 051-747-1051, broiled ribs.

Korea House: 646-3 Jungheung-dong, Buk-gu, 062-511-2121, tenderloin.

Daegu

Damsowon: 185-14 Daebong 1-dong, Jung-gu, 053-425-9688, traditional Korean dinner (TKD).

Silvillage: 732-2 Daebong 2-dong, Jung-gu, 053-421-1500, Galbi.

Hansol Garden: 1335-19 Pyeongri 4-dong, Sco-gu, 053-558-5555, Bulgogi.

Namgang Jangeo: 471-8 Nam-ri, Nonggong-eup, Dalseong-gun, 053-616-4040, marinated broiled eel.

Gwangju

Hotel Keumsoojang Arrirang House: 505-96 Gyerim-dong, Dong-gu, 062-525-2111,TKD.

Naksik Sutbulgui: 31-5 Gcum-dong, Dong-gu, 062-222-6489, Charcoaled pork ribs.

Daejeon

Goryeo Hoegwan: 223-8 Seonhwa-dong, Jung-gu, 042-257-4732, boiled rice in hot stone bowl.

Kkokko Center: 498 Wolpyeong 1-dong, Seo-gu, 042-525-5555, ginseng chicken soup.

Dunsan Jangeogui: 1500 Dunsan-dong, Seo-gu, 042-484-8545, broiled eel.

Doseong: 117-5 Birae-dong, Daedeok-gu, 042-672-5047, BBQ beef.

Incheon

Geosong: 193-12 Juan 1-dong, Nam-gu, 032-862-5511, beef ribs.

Darijib: 550-2 Okryeon-dong, Yeonsu-gu, 032-833-1796, crab soup.
New Core Myeonok: 3-2 Inhyeon-dong, Jung-gu, 032-766-4292,
beef ribs.

Ulsan

Okdol Gudeuljang Samgyeobsal: 178-2 Seongnam-dong, Jung-gu,
052-243-9906, grilled-sliced pork
Ijo Hanjeongsik: 878-4 Dal-dong, Nam-gu, 052-258-9000, TKD.

Jeonju

Han Guk gwan: 712-3 Geumam-dong, Deokjin-gu, 063-272-9229,
bibimbab (steamed rice, beef, & mixed vegetables in a bowl).
Banadolsotbab: 74-1 Jungang-dong 4-ga, Wasan-gu, 063-288-3174,
dolsotbab (rice mixed with vegetables and meat served in a hot stone
bowl).

Suwon

Suwon Yet Wanggalbi: 1014-1 Gwonseon-dong, Gwonseon-gu,
031-237-1257, galbi.
Sin Yeong Dong: 1115- Ingye-dong, Paldal-gu, 031-239-8155,
tenderloin.

Gangneung

Ttalbuja Makguksu: 561-3 Anin 2-ri, Gangdong-myeon,
033-644-6906, makguksu (noodle).
Sigol Halmeoni Chuotang: 297 Geumsan-ri, Seongsan-myeon,
033-644-8714, boiled mudfish soup.

Sokcho

Hwanghae Sikdang: 468-79 Jungang-dong, 033-633-3742, bulgogi.
Galbi Nara: 409-3 Nohak-dong, 033-632-8281, galbi.
Nojeok Bong: San 34-1 Daepo-dong, 033-636-2555, TKD.

Buyeo

Naruteo Sikdang: 7 Gugyo-ri, Buyeo-eup, 041-835-3155, Jangeogui (charcoiled eel).

Gudeurae Dolssambab: 96-2 Gua-ri, Buyeo-eup, 041-836-9259, dolsotbibimbab (steamed rice with assorted vegetables and grains in a hot bowl).

Seongsim Garden: 277-9 Dongnam-ri, Buyeo-eup, 041-835-2268, Dwaejigalbi (BBQ pork ribs).

Gongju

Seoul Restaurant: 716-1 Hakbong-ri, Banpo-myeon, 041-825-4195, Sanchaehanjeongsik (steamed rice with mountain vegetables)
Dotorimukchon: 643-7 Singwan-dong, 041-856-6963, dotorimuk (steamed rice with acorn jelly).

Gyeongju

Gamasote Jangjakbullo Sikdang: 319-2 Ha-dong, oribulgogi (BBQ duck).
Cheonma Sikdang: 185 Hwangnam-dong, 054-743-1995, samgyetang (ginseng chicken soup).

Jeju

Jungang Hoegwan: 283-1 Yeon-dong, 064-748-6311, Sagolujentang (bone & cabbage soup).
Geumneung Sikdang: 2051-1 Geumneung-ri, Hanlim-eup, Bukjeju-gun, 064-796-8400, haemuljeongol (boiled shellfish & seafood stew).

Ski Resorts in Korea

During the ski season, travel agencies operate buses; most of them are from Seoul. The average fees for ski rental range from 12,000 won to 32,000 won, and lift tickets range from 23,000 won to 42,000 won. Currently, Korea has 12 ski resorts: five in Gangwon-do province, five in Gyeonggi-do, one in Chungcheong Buk-do and one in Jeolla

Buk-do. In 2002, one U.S. dollar is equivalent to about 1,200 won. The following information provides websites, email addresses, telephone numbers, hotels/motels, and transportation from Seoul including costs of ski rentals and lifts.

Daemyung Vivaldi Park

Inquiries: Seoul office 02-2222-70445, local office 033-434-8311
www.daemyungcondo.com E-mail: tourseason@hanmail.net
Daemyung Vivaldi Park is 600m above sea level. It is often referred to as a beginner's paradise because of its 150m wide beginner's slope, but there are challenging runs, too.
Ski rental: full-day W30,000; half-day W23,000; night W23,000
Lift: full-day 38,000; half-day 29,000; night 29,000; full-day 42,000 wknd; half-day 33,000 wknd; night 33,000 wknd.
Amenities: 11 slopes, 9 lifts, 1 gondola, 1 sledding hill, bowling alley, golf course, night club, restaurants, sauna, game room.
Accommodations: Daemyung Vivaldi Park Condominium (1,090 rooms), Youth Hostel (188 rooms).
Transportation: Daemyung Travel 02-422-6677. A round-trip fare is W15,000.

Hyundai Sungwoo Resort

Inquiries: Seoul office; 02-3486-0432, local office; 033-340-3000
www.hdsungwoo.co.kr E-mail: webmaster@hdsungwoo.co.kr
Opened in December 1995, this gigantic year-round resort has many state-of-the-art facilities such as computerized snow making system, wave course, and mogul course.
Ski rental: full-day W22,000; half-day W18,000; night W18,000
Lift: full-day 38,000; half-day 29,000; night 29,000; full-day 42,000 wknd; half-day 33,000 wknd; night 33,000 wknd.
Amenities: 20 slopes, 8 lifts, 1 sledding hill, 1 gondola, golf course, indoor swimming pool, billiards, sauna, bowling alley, mini-theater, restaurants, fitness center, in-line skate park.

Accommodations: Hyundai Sungwoo Condominium (767 rooms), Youth Hostel (86 rooms).

Transportation: INET Tour 02-2215-8114

Attractions: Chiaksan Dream Land (25 min.), Chiaksan National Park (25 min.).

Jeollabuk-do Province

Jeollabuk-do Province has the biggest ski resort in Korea: Muju Resort. It was the venue of the 1997 Winter Universial and various international events. Jeollabuk-do Province has the biggest ski resort in Korea: Muju Resort. It was the venue of the 1997 Winter Universial and various international events.

Muju Resort

Inquiries: Seoul office; 02-3442-2055, local office; 063-322-9000. E-mail. muju-funski@hanmail.net

Set against the magnificent scenery of Deogyusan National Park, Muju is renowned for the spectacular scenery of Gucheondong Valley. As it is equipped with various auxiliary facilities such as a snow sleigh slope, outdoor hot springs, and an 18-hole golf course, even non-skiers can have a year-round great time. English ski lessons are available.

Ski rental: full-day W25,000; half-day W20,000; night W20,000

Lift: full-day 38,000; half-day 28,000; night 28,000; full-day 42,000 wknd; half-day 29,000 wknd; night 29,000 wknd.

Amenities: 26 slopes, 13 lifts, 1 sledding hill, 1 gondola, ski jumping park, mountain bike course, outdoor sauna, swimming pool, golf course, restaurants, nightclub.

Accommodations: Tirol Hotel (118 rooms), Family Hotel (974 rooms), Citizen Hotel (418 rooms).

Transportation: Daewon Express 02-2201-7710.

Attractions: Deogyusan National Park (15 min.), Muju Gucheondong Valley; Mt. Maisan (1 hr.).

Chungcheongbuk-do Province: Suanbo Sajo Resort
Inquiries: Seoul office; 02-3446-6021, local office; 043-846-0750
www.sajoresort.co.kr E-mail: sajo@sajoresort.co.kr

This family-oriented resort is situated in a splendid natural hot springs area, so visitors can enjoy both skiing and soaking in hot springs. Ski lessons in English are provided.
Ski rental: full day W12,000; half-day W8,000; night W8,000
Lift: full-day 35,000; half-day 25,000; night 25,000; full-day 37,000 wknd; half-day 27,000 wknd; night 27,000 wknd.
Amenities: 7 slopes, 3 lifts, 1 sledding hill, restaurants.
Accommodations: Sajo condominium (50 rooms), Youth Hostel (78 rooms).
Transportation: from Dong Seoul Bus Terminal to Suanbo.
Attractions: Woraksan National Park (25 min), Chungjuho Lake (40 min.), Danyang Palgyeong (eight scenic wonders of Danyang), Suanbo hot spings (5 min.).

Hot Springs
There are about 70 hot springs throughout Korea. Sauna rooms and bathing pools are made of materials believed to be good for the human body such as yellow clay, jade, elvan, or hinoki wood-features that cannot be found elsewhere. A variety of affiliated facilities are often included such as saunas, sleeping rooms, swimming pools, fitness centers, and open-air pools. Admission fee is usually W5,000 to W10,000.

Gangwon-do Province: Sorak Waterpia
It is located in Sokcho, known for the Seoraksan mountains. Sorak Waterpia is more than just a spa, but a huge hot spring theme park. There is an outdoor hot spring bathing pool where one can relax in naturally heated waters while enjoying a view of the East Sea. The place is notable for its dramatic artificial wave pool. More than 3,000

tons of hot spring water at 49C is supplied from underground every day. Call: 033-635-7700.

Jeollad-do Province: Jirisan Spa Land
The spa, a brand new hot springs, is located in Jirisan National Park in the southern Province. The spa has a cave sauna, swimming pool, and outdoor spa. Its germanium spring water is effective for skin care, anti-aging and neuralgia.
Transportation: Public transportation is available from Seoul Express Terminal.
Accommodation: Jirisan Spa Land, 061-783-2900.

Gyeonggi-do Province: Hot Springs in Ildong Pocheon
There are several hot springs in close proximity in Pocheon. They are Dragon Sulfur (031-536-4600), Saipan (031-536-2000), Jeil Sulfur Spring (031-536-6000), Hawaii (031-536-5000). These spas are known for their excellent facilities and water quality.
Transportation: Public transportation is available from Dong Seoul Bus Terminal.
Attractions: Traditional Liquor Meseum (brewery), Bears Town Ski Resort, golf courses and National Arboretum.

Chungcheong-do Province: Yuseong Hot Springs
The hot mineral water contains calcium, potassium, radium, sulfates and carbonates, and is said to be good for many ailments including neuralgia. This area is designated as "Yuseong Special Tourism Zone."
Transportation: Public transportation is available from Seoul Express Bus Terminal.
Accommodations: Riviera, 042-823-2111; Yuseong, 042-822-0811; Hongin, 042-822-2000; Expo 042-824-0035; Adria, 042-824-0211.
Attractions: Expo Park, Gyeryongsan National Park, and Currency Museum.

Gyeongsang-do Province: **Dongnae Hot Springs**
One of the oldest spas in Korea. The water contains abundant magnesium, and the temperature is around 55°C. Hur Shim Chung is famous for its hot bath resort equipped with various baths.
Transportation: from Busan, use Busan subway line 1.
Accommodations: Hur Shim Chung Spa, 051-555-1121; Nokcheon Spa, 051-555-4823.

Shops and Markets
Insa-dong: antique shops, art galleries and old book stores.
Chang-anpyong Antique Market: paintings, calligraphy, old chests, stone artifacts, ceremics and lacquerware.
Kyongdong Market: oriental medicine
Hwanghak-dong Flea Market: brass bowls, cutlery, jewelry and old Korean wide-brimmed hats
Yongsan Electronics Market: electronic goods

Departmental Stores
Galleria Tel 3449-4114. **Hyundai** Tel 320-3000/552-2233. **Hamilton Hotel Shopping Center** Tel 794-0174. **Hanshin Core** Tel 978-1919. **Hunyoung Omni** Tel 971-9000. **Lotte** Tel 771-2500/2632-2500/966-2500, www.department.lotte.co.kr. **Printemps** Tel 774-5111. **Midopa** Tel 754-2222/960-2222.

Night Clubs
There is a range of night clubs located in hotels, but these are expensive. Alternatively, visit the clubs in the Yongdong and Itaewon areas, the latter catering to largely foreign clientele.
Nightclubs, bars and casinos at the following hotels: **Sheraton Walker Hill** Tel 456-2121. **Olympos** Tel 762-5181. **Cheju Grand** Tel 064-743-2121. **Cheju Oriental** Tel 064-751-5599.

Korean Traditional Music and Dance Performances

National Center for Korean Performing Arts Tel 580-3040. **Chongdong Theater** Tel 773-8960, www.chongdong.com. **Seoul Nori Madang** Tel 410-3410. **Sejong Cultural Center** Tel 399-1516. **Pusan Cultural Center** Tel 051-623-0179. **Chindo Regional Culture Center** Tel 0632-544-3710.

TRANSPORT AND COMMUNICATIONS
Access Codes

Country code 82, **City code** 2 (for Seoul), Dial 0 first when making international calls from Korea. Direct international calls begin with 001, followed by the country code, area code and local number.

Telephone Service Numbers

Local Telephone Directory Assistance 114. **International Dialing Assistance** 0074. **International Telephone Operator** 0077. **English Speaking Operator in Seoul** 211-0114.

E-mail and Internet Service Providers

AT&T/Unitel (Samsung) Tel 080-500-5588, www.att.co.kr/ www.unitel.co.kr. **Chollian** Tel 106 (free call), www.chollian.net. **Hanaro Telecom** www.hanaro.com. **Nextel** (available in Seoul only) Tel (02) 536-9900, www.uriel.net.

Bus, Train and Taxi Information

Airport Express Buses Tel 665-1094/662-2859 provide transportation between Kimpo International Airport and downtown Seoul. **To book a cab**: Tel 3431-5100.

Car rental services: **Eagle** Tel 332-4422. **Han Gang** Tel 2247-0022. **Jangwon** Tel 556-8177. **Jeil** Tel 733-8887. **Korea Express** Tel 719-7295. **Hertz** Tel 3780-8600. **Samsung** Tel 662-7100. **Saehan** Tel 896-0031. **Seoul** Tel 474-0011.

Subway Information: www.lifeinkorea.com/information/trns/
subways.cfm

MEDIA

Newspapers
There are two English newspapers: **The Korea Times**
www.koreatimes.com. **Korea Herald** www.koreaherald.com.
Check out these websites for the English version of the following
Korean newspapers: **Dong-A** www.donga.com. **Chosun**
www.chosun.com. **Joongang** www.joins.com.

Television and Radio Channels
Korea has five TV networks: KBS1, KBS2, MBC, SBC and EBS. In
addition, channels on cable TV bring in a wide variety of programs
from news, entertainment to tourist information. Korea has eight
radio stations. including AFKN, the U.S. military station on 1530 AM
and 102.7 FM in Seoul.

LANGUAGE INSTITUTES
Ewha Women's University Tel 312-0067. **Hankuk University of
Foreign Studies** Tel 961-4174. **Sogang University** Tel 701-8963.
Yonsei University Tel 361-3466.

BUSINESS INFORMATION

Business Opportunities in Korea
For partner search, business opportunities, and investment opportunities, see **Korea Trade-Investment Promotion Agency (KOTRA)**,
www.kotra.or.kr. **Korea Investment Service Center** www.kisc.org;
kisc@kotra.or.kr. **American Chamber of Commerce in Korea** Tel
82-2-564-2040. **The European Union Chamber of Commerce in**

Korea www.eucck.org. **The Korea Chamber of Commerce & Industry** 45 Namdaemunno 4-ga, Chung-gu, Seoul, Tel 316-3114. puter Press, 1982.

This is a useful book for learning the basics of the Korean alphabet (*hangul*) and language. Beginners' vocabulary and grammar are taught through the use of relevant dialogue, such as riding in a taxi, buying something at the market, and going to the doctor.

BUDGET INNS AND RESTAURANTS

Korea National Tourism Organization operates the Korea Budget Inns Reservation Center (K-BIRC) to serve expatriates for low prices. K-BIRC provides free information and reservation assistance on budget inns and restaurants in 15 major tourist destinations. Facilities and service levels differ from inn to inn and restaurant to restaurant, as well as their ability to speak foreign languages, but they will all give visitors a warm welcome and fine hospitality.

K-BIRC: **www.visitkorea.or.kr**; Tel 82-2-757-0086; Fax 82-2-319-0086; and address-Tourist Information Center, 10 Dad-dong, Jung-gu, Seoul 100-180 Korea. Business hours: open M-F 9 am-8 pm, but from Nov. to Feb. 9 am-7 pm.

How to make reservations

To make a reservation, submit a Budget Inns Reservation Request Form on the K-BIRC website–**www.visitkorea.or.kr**. and print, fill it out, and mail or fax the form to K-BIRC. Or, send an email to kntotic@knto.or.kr. A reservation confirmation will be sent via email, fax, or mail.

Major credit cards such as visa, master card, diners club, American Express, and JCB card are accepted at most hotels and restaurants in major cities. The Korea National Tourism Organization (KNTO) has provided the following information.

Budget Inns

Budget inns comprise of yeogwans, which are Korean style inns.. Other classes of inns are usually call hotels, jangs or motels. Yeogwang rooms are generally heated in the winter and have beds, private bathrooms with hot water, air-conditioners and other amenities.

The following are useful phrases at a hotels, motels, and budget inns:

Do you have any vacancy?
Bin-bang isummnika?
No, we don't.
Aniyo, op-sumnida.
What hotel can I call for a room?
O-nu hotel-ae chon-hwa halkayo?
I would like to stay 1, 2 or 3 nights.
Il-, ee-, sam-baak hago sipseumnida.
I would like a room with a bed.
Chim-dae-baang eul wonhamnida.
I would like to have a quiet room.
Joyonghan baang eul jooseyo.
I want a room with a nice view.
Jeonmaang-e joeun baang-eul jooseyo.
When is the check out time?
Towsil sigaan-eun myot-simnika?
Is a shower available in the bathroom?
Hwajangsil-ae shower itseumnika?
Is there a bathtub in the bathroom?
Hwajangsil-ae yokjo-neun itseumnika?
I would like to switch my room.
Baang-eul baakugo sipeumnida.
Please give me a wake-up call 7 in the morning.
Aachim ilgop sie kkaewo juseyo.
Can I use my credit card?
Sinyong card-reul sayong halsu itseumnika?

Could you show me a nearest subway station?
Gaakkaun jihacheol yeok-eul gaarucheo juseyo.
Would you please call a taxi for me?
Taeksee-reul bulleo juseyo.
How can I make an international call?
Gukje jeonhwa haago sipseumnida.
Are there any tourist attractions nearby?
Geuncheo-ae jo-eun gwangwangji-ga itsemnika?

Budget Inns by Cities

Seoul

Samo Motel: (02) 739-0604, fax (02) 739-0609. 46-10 Susong-dong, Jongno-gu. Location: neaby Gyeonbokgung palace and Biwon.
City Hotel: (02) 744-4197. 24-1, Unni-dong, Jongno-gu. Location: nearby Changdeokgung palace.
Trek Korea Guest House: (02) 743-7631, fax (02) 743-7632. 78-3 Hyehwa-dong, Jongno-gu. Location: nearby Changgyeonggung palace.
Hotel Greenfield: (02) 699-1314. 1105-12 Hwagok 6-dong, Gangseo-gu. Location: nearby Gimpo International Airport.
Grand Hotel: (02) 417-7534. 42-8 Bangi-dong, Songpa-gu. Location: nearby Olympic Park.

Busan

More Hotel: (051) 243-9360, fax (051) 243-9351. 235 Amnam-dong, Seo-gu. Location: Songdo Beach area.
Cheonil Oncheon Hotel: (051) 553-8192, fax (051) 553-8190. 142 Oncheon 1-dong, Dangnae-gu. Location: Dongnae Hot Springs area.
Ramere Hotel: (051) 504-0523. 1447-3 Oncheon 3-dong, Dongnae-gu. Location: Dongnae Hot Springs area.
Park Hotel: (051) 755-5005, fax (051) 755-5010. 201-1 Gwangan 2-dong, Suyeong-gu. Location: Gwanglli Beach area.

Angel Hotel: (051) 802-8223, fax (051) 802-2262. 223-2 Bujeon-dong, Busanjin-gu.Location: Downtown area.

Daegu
Samujang: (053) 422-5121. 149-92 Samdoek 2-ga, Jung-gu. Location: nearby Daegu Railway Station.
Royal Park Jang: (053) 744-8247. 379-4 Sincheon 4-dong, Dong-gu. Location: nearby the Express Bus Terminal.

Gwanju
Motel Ramada: (062) 363-4403. 15-5 Gwangcheon-dong, Seo-gu. Location: nearby the Express Bus Terminal.
Booyoung: (062) 573-2233. 45-22 Maegok-dong, Buk-gu. Location: nearby Korea Trade Center.

Daejeon
Hyatt Motel: (042) 585-8895. 332-16 Yucheon-dong, Jung-gu. Location: nearby Seobu Bus Terminal.
Vienna Motel: (042) 823-7337. 548-4 Bongmyeong-dong, Yuseong-gu. Location: Yuseong Hot Spring area.

Incheon
Yangji Motel: (032) 873-1339. 230-11 Juan 1-dong, Nam-gu. Location: nearby Juan Railway Station.
White Palace: (032) 887-8228. 630-24 Yonghyeon 5-dong, Nam-gu. Location: nearby Yeonan wharf.

Ulsan
Mirabo Motel: (052) 260-7114. 1475-12 Samsan-dong, Nam-gu. Location: nearby Express Bus Terminal.
Ariana: (052) 239-9966. 83-11 Jinha-ri, Seosaeng-myeon, Ulju-gun Location: Jinha Beach area.

Jeonju

Taegeukjang Motel: (063) 245-8700. 858-5 Sanjeong-dong, Deokjin-gu. Location: nearby Jeonju Railway Station.
Sydney Motel: (063) 255-3311. 700-3 Geumam-dong, Deokjin-gu. Location: nearby the Express Bus Terminal.

Suwon

Galleria Motel: (031) 225-3007. 1014-8 Gwonseon-dong, Gwonseon-gu. Location: nearby City Hall.
Dongsan Hotel: (031) 238-9371, fax (031) 238-9378. 940-7 Ingye-dong, Paldal-gu. Location: nearby Dongsuwon Hospital.

Gangneung

Victoria Park: (033) 644-2665. 107-5 Anhyeon-dong. Location: Gyeongpo Beach area.
New Grand Hotel: (033) 646 8181. 156-24 Gyo-dong. Location: Downtown area.

Sokcho

Suyeon Motel: (033) 636-6642. 986-6 Gyo-dong. Location: Downtown area.
Choksan Hot Spring Resort: (033) 636-4000, fax (033) 636-4007. 972-1 Nohak-dong. Location: nearby Mt. Seorak National Park.

Buyeo

Motel Arirang: (041) 832-5656, fax (041) 832-5657. 295 Gua-ri, Buyeo-eup. Location: nearby Jeongnimsaji downtown area.
Crystal Motel: (041) 835-1717. 121-5 Gwanbuk-ri, Buyeo-eup. Location: nearby Mt. Busosan.

Gongju

Eden Park: (041) 856-0876. 594-10 Singwan-dong. Location: nearby Express Bus Terminal.

Wonang Park: (041) 857-8989. 594-11 Singgwan-dong. Location: nearby Express Bus Terminal.

Gyeongju

Mokhwa House: (054) 743-0990. 121-6 Noseo-dong. Location: nearby Kim Yu-sin's Tomb.

Baekman Jang: (054) 745-6781. 458-6 Gujeong-dong. Location: nearby Bulkuksa Temple.

Bomun Silla Jang: (054) 745-1214. 242-11 Sinpyeong-dong. Location: at the Bomun Lake Resort.

Jeju-do

Juju Core Hotel: (064) 744-6600, fax (064) 747-7001. 304-13 Yeon-dong. Location: nearby Jeju International Airport.

Starseong Motel: (064) 763-4677. 308-5 Seogwi-dong, Seogwipo. Location: nearby Cheonjiyeon Falls.

FURTHER READING

Living in Korea

Living in Korea. Richard B. Rucci, Seoul International Publishing House, 1987.

• This book gives comprehensive, updated information about everything from planning your move to Korea to shopping in Korea and what to do and see. Many indispensable phone numbers are included.

Korean Culture

Korean Patterns. Paul Crane, Seoul, Kwangjin Publishing Co., 1978.

• This book was first published in 1967, by a medical missionary to Korea. It is a classic in understanding the way Koreans think and act. Since it was written over 20 years ago, it describes an earlier Korea, but many of the customs are still practised.

Looking at Each Other. Marion E. Current and Dong-ho Choi, Seoul, Seoul International Publishing House, 1983.

• Humorous illustrations and short descriptions contrast Korean culture with Western cultures.

Through a Rain Spattered Window. Michael Daniels, Seoul, Taewon Publishing Company, 1973.

• The author of this book lived in Korea for 15 years. The book is a collection of insightful essays on topics such as the family, time and weather, and Confucian tradition.

Korea, An Introduction. James Hoare and Susan Pares, Kegan Paul International Limited, London 1988.
• A comprehensive introduction to many aspects of Korea, including politics and history, culture, social structure and the spiritual side.

Korean Cultural Potpourri. Kyu-tae Jeon, Seoul, Seoul International Publishing House, 1987.
• This book is a series of articles, originally published in the English-language newspaper, *The Korean Herald.* They are interesting and well-written, explaining Korean culture from a Korean's perspective.

Women of Korea. Yung Chung Kim, Editor, Seoul, Ewha Woman's University Press, 1976.
• This is an introduction to the history of Korea from ancient times to 1945, paying particular notice to Korean women. The details about individuals' lives make it fascinating to read.

Crosscurrents. Susan Pares, Seoul, Seoul International Publishing House, 1985.
• This is a collection of articles originally written for *The Korean Herald.* The author is an expatriate who writes about some of the joys and sorrows of living in Korea.

Communication Styles in Two Different Cultures: Korean and American. Myung Seok Park, Seoul, Han Shin Publishing Co., 1979.
• This book gives some theoretical background on intercultural communication, and then highlights some of the difficulties of communication between Koreans and Americans. Some of the examples are quite entertaining

A Guide to Korean Cultural Heritage. The Korean Overseas Culture and Information Services, Hollym, 1998.
• This book provides in-depth details about traditional Korean cultural practices.

Proverbs, East and West. Compiled by Kim Young-chol, Hollym, 1991.
• An anthology of Chinese, Korean and Japanese sayings, which provide a delightful window into understanding these different ways of thinking.

Korean Business
Korean Etiquette and Ethics in Business. Boye De Mente, NTC Business Books, Chicago, 1988.
• For the business person, this book covers everything from the personal nature of business to Korean unions and advertising barriers.

Intercultural Communication
The Art of Crossing Cultures. Craig Storti, Intercultural Press Inc., Yarmouth, ME, USA, 1990.
• This book explains the phenomenon of culture shock in depth and gives practical advice on how to make the adjustment.

Korean Cooking
Traditional Korean Cuisine. Woul Young Chu, Los Angeles, Jai Min Chang, *The Korea Times,* L.A., 1985
• A nicely illustrated cookbook, with clear, easy-to-follow recipes. There is a section on table settings and table manners.

Tourism in Korea

Insight Guides: Korea. Apa Productions (Hong Kong) Ltd., 1984.
• This book provides sensitive, in-depth information on a variety of Korean topics. An extensive travel section is included. The photographs are reason enough to buy this guide.

Korea. Korea National Tourism Corporation, Seoul, 1985.
• General information about Korea is included with this basic travel guide. Maps and photographs are included.

Korean Language

Modern Conversational Korean. Suk-in Chang, Seoul, Seoul Com

THE AUTHORS

Ben and Sonja met in 1978 in Minneapolis, Minnesota. Ben had just completed his Ph.D. at the University of Iowa. Sonja had just finished her B.A. in Sociology at St Olaf College; she later went on to complete an M.A. in Social Work at the University of Chicago in 1981. The two were married in June 1982, after which they moved to South Korea, Ben's native country.

After living in Korea for seven years, the authors returned to the United States. Ben does research, writing and consulting in the areas of Cross-cultural Communication and Health Behavior. Sonja completed her Ph.D. in Social Work and Social Research at Portland State University in June 2002. She is an associate professor of social work at Concordia University in Portland, Oregon. She also does consulting for businesses in Korea.

INDEX